Sailing Through Troubled Waters
Christianity in the Middle East

Mitri Raheb

First Edition

Sailing Through Troubled Waters

Christianity in the Middle East

Mitri Raheb

Copy right © 2013 Diyar Publisher
ISBN : 13: 978-1484947067
ISBN-10: 1484947061

Printing press: Latin Patriarchate
Art direction : Diyar Publisher
Designer : Engred Anwar Al-Khoury
Supported by : Bright Stars of Bethlehem

All rights reserved. Except for brief quotations in critical articles or reviews, no part of this book may be reproduced in any manner without prior written permission from the publisher.

1.Theology - Middle East 2. Palestine 3. Arab Christianity 4. Liberation 5. Islam - Qur'an 6. Theology – History - Politics

w w w . d i y a r . p s

Contents

Foreword 7

1. **Christianity and Religious Plurality in the Middle East: A Historical overview** 9

2. **Christianity in the Arabian Peninsula from the End of the Sixth to the Seventh Century** 27

3. **Contextualizing the Scripture:** 49
   Towards a New Understanding of the Qur'an.
   An Arab Christian Perspective

4. **The Evangelical Lutheran Church in Jordan and the Holy Land: Past and Present** 77

5. **The Situation of the Palestinian Christian Community in the Holy Land** 93

6. **The Revolution in the Arab World: Towards a Public Theology of Liberation** 105

7. **Human Rights in the Middle East and North Africa: The Situation of the Christians** 117

Endnotes 125

Bibliography 138

Foreword

It was in 1988 that Mitri Raheb was ordained Pastor in the Evangelical Lutheran Church of Jordan and the Holy Land and was installed as Pastor of the Evangelical Lutheran Christmas Church in Bethlehem after finishing his seminary studies and doctorate in Germany in Church History. Besides being a Pastor, Mitri Raheb continued to be involved in the theological discussion and research both at home as well as in regional and international settings. The selected articles were given by Rev. Raheb at several occasions. The first article on Christianity and Religious plurality was given at Fuller Seminary in 2003 during the author sabbatical as Mission Partner in Residence with the PCUSA. The second and third articles on the political and ecclesiastical context in the Arab Peninsula during the 6-7th centuries were part of a Post doctoral research that the author did during his stay at Harford Seminary in Connecticut. The funding for the research leading to these papers was provided by a scholarship from the Research Enablement Program, a grant for mission scholarship supported by the Pew Charitable Trusts. Philadelphia, Pennsylvania and administered by the Overseas Ministries Study Center, New Haven, Connecticut. The article on the History of the Evangelical Lutheran Church in Jordan and the Holy Land is a summary of the author's doctoral dissertation at Marburg University and of his German book "Das reformatorische Erbe unter den palaestinensern" published by Guetrsloh in 1990. The article on the Situation of the Palestinian Christian community in the Holy Land was given as lecture to several church delegation interested in the situation of the Christians of the Holy land, while the article on the Arab Spring was given at a regional conference in Lebanon. The last chapter of the book is different in nature since it is actually a short lecture given at a hearing at the Danish Parliament, Christiansburg, in Copenhagen on May 21st 2012.

    Diyar publisher is happy to publish these mostly unpublished articles of Rev. Dr. Mitri Raheb to coincide with his silver ordination in May 2013. Special thanks go to Mrs. Sarah Bailey – Makari for doing such a great job in editing this book and for doing it in a short and timely manner. Our thanks go also to Mrs. Hiba Nasser – Atrash for typing and manuscript and for Ms. Angela Joy Rogers for assisting with the footnotes and bibliography. The publication of this book would not have been possible without the support of Bright Start of Bethlehem in the USA. Our hope is that this book will provide the readers with new insights into the work of Mitri Raheb as well as of Christianity in the Middle East.

Diyar Publisher
May 2013

1.
Christianity and Religious Plurality in the Middle East

A Historical overview

The Middle East is the region of origin of Christianity and Islam, as well as Judaism. I will concentrate my reflections in this paper mainly on Christianity and to some extend Islam as they developed and interacted in the Middle East throughout the centuries.

A Historical Overview
Christianity in the first three centuries

From the beginning two characteristics were central in the development of Christianity:

- Christianity developed in a context of enormous religious plurality. From its start it had to learn to navigate within this plurality and to find its way relating to its Jewish roots, while at the same time distinguishing itself from those same roots. The new Christian faith developed in continuity and simultaneously in discontinuity to its Jewish roots. Christianity, from the beginning, also related to different Roman and Greek religions and philosophies, in various ways, ranging from utilizing and adopting some of their beliefs to a harsh critique of those religions. One example being the relationships developed to the Samaritans, Gnosis, and the sermon of Paul in Athens(Acts 17:16-34), etc.

- Christianity developed as a pluralistic phenomenon. From its early days two distinctive congregations developed and existed side by side in Jerusalem; one for the believers, from a Palestinian context, and a second for believers from a Hellenistic context(Acts 6). From the day of its birth at Pentecost the Christian faith in Jesus Christ proved to be not only sensitive to cultural and linguistic differences, but was also a faith which related to, interacted with, critiqued and embraced various cultural and linguistic expressions.

Christianity in the fourth to the sixth century

These two characteristics were present and continued to shape the Christian faith through the first three centuries. Yet this situation changed during the fourth and fifth centuries in two ways:

- With Constantine's conversion to Christianity and with the declaration of Christianity as the official and later only recognized religion of the empire, religious plurality was soon seen as something to be fought rather than tolerated in a Christian empire. Unorthodox belief came to be seen as a direct challenge to the emperor's authority to Church unity and thus as a threat to the stability of the state. However, the Byzantine Empire was not able to end the religious plurality of the Middle East as the Samaritan revolt; wars with the Berbers, Donatists and many others clearly show.

- The special interaction between Gospel and culture led to the development of diverse national churches in the Middle East. The concept of a national church meant that a specific group of people, with a distinctive historical identity, language and culture adopted the Christian faith, which became woven into and a part of their new identity. This was true for the Armenian, Jacobite, Coptic and Ethiopian Churches and the Apostolic Church of the East known as the Nestorian Church, and it was also true for the Melkite Church, the official Greek Church of the Byzantine Empire. This very diversity of Christian churches in the Middle East was highly unique characteristic for the formation of the Christian faith in diverse "national" settings of the region. Within the Roman Empire these embryonic national churches were more or less equal before a heathen political authority. With the conversion of Constantine to Christianity and with the formation of a Byzantine Empire, the Greek national church became what was known later as the Melkite Church, or the Church of the Emperor. The Emperor and his church, however, grew uncomfortable with the existence of other national churches within the boundaries of the empire, as they comprised a large portion of the populations of Egypt and Syria and existed throughout the East. A great concern for each of the Byzantine emperors was this diversity within Christianity. The interaction between Gospel and culture in forming these national Christian identities was neglected. The main concern was to find a sort of Christian uniformity that could underline the emperor's authority and provide some kind of stability for the newly formed "Christian Empire," which was threatened from outside by non-Christian political powers, the Persian in the east, and other heathen powers in the north. The focus of most of the so-called "ecumenical councils" was largely on finding some uniformity. Yet, no emperor and none of the councils succeeded in solving this issue. All attempts to unite these embryonic national identities behind a theological compromise and/or formula were unsuccessful because they did not understand the special interaction of Gospel and culture. On the contrary, these attempts fostered the developments of these identities into established "national churches." The non-Greek "national churches" were declared non-Kosher or un-orthodox. There were eras in which those "monophysite" churches were tolerated, and times when they were persecuted, the harshest persecution taking place under the ultra-orthodox Justin II(565-578). In spite of these many peaceful and violent attempts, Christianity remained diverse and pluralistic in nature as well as theologically. Politically speaking one of those churches became the church of the Emperor and thus held power, while all other churches were deprived of political power except the "grassroots power" provided by their followers.

Christianity in the early Islamic period

This, for all intents and purposes, was the religious landscape in which Islam largely developed and expanded.

- The Prophet Muhammad, a trader by profession, was acquainted with the two existing national-religious superpowers of his time, a Christian Byzantine to the west and a Zoroastrian-Persian one to the east, as well as with some of the diverse "national churches." In another chapter I'm arguing that one can trace several developments in the self-understanding of the Prophet Muhammad. "In the Meccan period one can see the Qur'an as a warning to the people of Mecca, Muhammad as a prophet to the Arabs, and the Qur'an as an Arab-Judeo-Christian liturgy. A positive attitude towards the Jewish and Christian scriptures in particular can be observed during this period. In the Madinan period, the Qur'an distinguishes itself increasingly from the previous scriptures and begins to function as a criterion by which the former are judged. It is a revelation to the "pagans"- those outside the Judeo-Christian Heilsgeschichte, and a cultic law for the newly established Muslim community."

- This process of differentiation between Islam and the earlier religions of Judaism and Christianity did not occur solely at the level of theological debate. The debate itself was set in the context of the expansion of the Muslim community in Medina as the Medinian Arab tribes converted en masse to Muhammad's teaching. Islam was rapidly becoming a unique community, an Arab national religion. The more this religion was able to expand geographically, the more it developed as a new third regional "Arabian" Empire and later even an international power, whose socio-political and religious identity was rooted in the Prophet Muhammad's religious teaching.

- The expansion of this Arab-Islamic Empire throughout the Middle East brought with it a major change for the Christian national churches and the other religions and sects in the region. Unlike the Byzantine Empire, this newly established and expanding Arab-Islamic Empire did not see the religious and confessional plurality of the Middle East as a threat. The Byzantine and Persian Empires, as political entities, were perceived as threats but not necessarily as religious communities. Thus Islam, the religion which is often described as a religion that does not distinguish between "State and Church" was capable of distinguishing between both entities in its relation to the other monotheistic religious communities. The new empire, within less than a century, was able to occupy crucial parts of the Byzantine Empire and to push it to the north, while also occupying the Persian Empire and converting it to Islam. For the Christian national churches within the dar-as-Silm (House of Peace meaning the territories under Islamic rule) this new development was perceived in different ways. For the Melkite Church it was a real threat, a humiliating defeat, and a deprivation of political power. For the other monophysite churches this was welcomed with relief. Their orthodoxy was not questioned. The new empire respected its "religio-national" identities as long as they in turn accepted the political supremacy of the empire. Since those churches were deprived of political power anyway, under the Byzantine Empire, this new situation did not change that reality. The new empire knew how to utilize the hate and fear of different religious groups and the monophysite national churches toward the Byzantine Empire to its own advantage. It needed them to build and administer an ever-expanding empire. As time passed, Islam developed the millet system in order to integrate Judaism and Christianity into the empire. Millet means "a community or a nation of people with a particular religion." Every recognized millet was given the right to use its own rites, as well as the right to maintain its own court and institutions. The millet system was based on a concept of "autonomy" or "self-governance" of religio-national communities within a larger Islamic political empire. Religious plurality was tolerated as long as there was recognition of the political unity and supremacy of the Muslim Empire.

- For the existing national churches of the Middle East this new reality in the seventh century meant that from then on they found themselves in a third context which differed from that of the first three or the 4-6 centuries. Christians now had to relate to another religion called Islam. Two important movements can be depicted vis-à-vis this new relationship. There were several diverse attempts as well as theological apologetic literature to defend their faith, not their orthodoxy. Although Islam recognized the Christians as ahl al-kitab(the people of the Book), there were many attacks by several Muslim preachers on the basic Christian beliefs of Trinity, Incarnation and Salvation. As in the first three centuries, when Christians needed to defend their faith in a context of Roman paganism and Greek philosophy, from now on they needed to do so in an Islamic context. In addition to this apologetic movement another movement took root developed by the Christians of the Middle East relating to the new religion, Islam, which was in fact nothing but an Arab national religion. It interrupted the formation of a national Arab Church to form a new Arab religion, which expanded rapidly, beyond the Arab Peninsula and thus became a "universal religion." The Arabic language and Arab culture remained a crucial component of the new religion. This contextual religion underwent a major change when its particular Arab cultural component was universalized. In this respect the relationship of the Qur'an and culture developed differently from that of Gospel and culture. Christians were used to relating the Gospel of Jesus Christ to diverse cultures. From this point on, however, there were many attempts by Middle Eastern Christians to relate to the Arab culture of the new religion by writing theology in Arabic. Those Christians learned to distinguish the cultural components of the new empire from its distinct religious component, thus embracing the cultural and disagreeing with the religious.

- Islam did not only interrupt the formation of a national Arab church, it also interrupted the entire missionary movement of forming other potential national churches in the new empire. From now on any potential formation of new national churches in North Africa or in Asia was no longer possible. The whole missionary impact of the Apostolic Church of the East known as the Nestorian Church, which as early as the 7th century reached as far as China was lost, with the exception of the Church of South India and the Maronite Church. The latter wasn't truly a new formation, but a reformation of an existing Aramaic Phoenician Church.

New national church formations would from now on take place in the northern and eastern hemispheres within Slavic, Germanic, and other cultures.

- From its beginnings, Islam made clear that it does not tolerate any mission efforts among followers or tribes, as if the "theology of apostasy" of the Byzantine Empire was adopted by Islam and became the norm. This meant a kind of stagnation for the existing national churches. Hence the main concern of these churches became survival rather than expansion and growth. Their distinctive character as national churches helped them to preserve their identity, yet, at the same time, the missionary dynamism and vitality of these churches was lost and replaced by a more static reality.

- The mission of these national churches was to become a totally different and an unexpected one. Since the relationship of Islam to culture was different from that of Christianity, and since the Qur'an did not need to be translated into other languages, the vitality and dynamism of the new empire was at stake. The Arabian Peninsula, the homeland of the new empire, was until the seventh century a quiet and remote corner of the world. Historical events and cultural developments took place far from the region. The new empire was incapable of sustaining itself, developing, or expanding, unless it could relate to the former cultural achievements of the Romans, Greeks, etc. In this context, the mission of the national churches was to be the bridge between those two unrelated worlds. It was the linguistic capabilities and more importantly the deep understanding of cultural formations which made it possible for followers of some of these national churches to translate major works of philosophy and science from Greek and Latin into Arabic, thus making them available to the new Arab Muslim Empire. A few centuries later it was the mission of followers of the same national churches to make the philosophical, medical, and scientific inheritance of the Arab Islamic Empire available to Europe. Furthermore, during the 19th century, and for the third time in history, followers of the same national churches were called to shake the Middle East out of its deep medieval sleep, promoting the renaissance of Arab culture and language and introducing modernity to the region.

Christianity during the Crusaders Era

While the national churches of the Middle East continued to live in a Christian pluralistic setting as well as within a non-Christian Muslim context, the Church in the north developed two separate rival mono-Christian and confessional cultures: Catholic in the northwest and orthodox in the northeast. Where the latter was more open to national-cultural formations within Orthodoxy(Russian, Romanian, etc.), the Latin Empire and Church remained in total uniformity until the Reformation. Eastern and Western Christian powers alike were dissatisfied with the fact that Islam continued to occupy land once belonging to the Byzantine Empire. Both entities understood themselves as the heirs of ancient Byzantine. And they were truly inheritors of the same exclusive attitude that is adverse to Christian diversity and religious plurality. The Crusades thus introduced a new situation to the Middle East. Among the Muslims, they created a deep and complex fear that the West did not acknowledge the reality of Islam controlling major parts of the former Byzantine Empire, something which was accepted by the national churches within the Muslim Empire. The way in which the Crusades treated the Christians of the Middle East created a deep suspicion among the existing national churches that the days of persecution under a monolithic Christian Empire might return. From then on there was a major decline in the Christian presence in the Middle East, resulting in a Christian majority becoming a minority. And although the national churches in the Middle East suffered immensely under the Crusades, like the Muslims, there was also a growing fear among Muslims, especially after the assumption of power by the Muslim Moguls, that the existence of national churches might constitute a threat to the stability of the Muslim Empire.

Christianity in the nineteenths and twentieth centuries

Another intervention by "the West" in the Middle East, provoked by Napoleon's invasion in 1799, brought major developments regarding the role of Christians in the Muslim Empire. During the era of Muhammad Ali, 1831-1839, the Middle East experienced far-reaching change: New concepts of nationalism and secularism were introduced to the region, resulting later in the collapse of the Ottoman Empire, the formation of mini national states, and the development of a new equation between Christians and Muslims. National identities started replacing the national churches' identities as well as to some extent Muslim religious identity. It was argued that national unity was necessary in order for Christians and Muslims to transcend their religious differences. This process led to the transformation of religion into a mere personal and intimate relationship between the individual and God, something foreign to both the concepts of a national church and of an Islamic Empire. The religious plurality of the region was based henceforth on a national and geographical unity while the notion of a religious identity was replaced by national identity. Never the less the replacement was not genuine. What worked in Europe or in North America proved often not to work in the Middle East. Likewise, the model of communism/socialism neither worked/succeeded in Europe nor in the Middle East.

The different concepts of nationalism, secularism and socialism were unable to provide satisfactory solutions to the issues of religious, national and cultural diversities, and were also unable to provide political stability, economic prosperity and civil liberties.

Christianity in the Middle East today

This crisis in the Middle East is felt and expressed in two parallel socio-religious phenomena. On the one hand there is a growing Muslim resurgence and fundamentalism and on the other a Christian and to a lesser extent also Muslim wave of immigration out of the region to the West and North. Yet the consequences of these parallel phenomena are not the same. While Islam through its resurgence and expansion outside of dar as-Silm, and the petro-dollar, developed within the space of a century into a major global power, the emigration of Middle Eastern Christians threatens to erase national churches from the lands of their origin. William Dalrymple in his book, From the Holy Mountain, traces the footsteps of a middle aged monk's journey from Arthos to Eqypt, showing how Christianity is almost disappearing from Turkey, Syria, Jordan, Palestine and even Lebanon, and might not survive the 21st century except in Egypt. Many of the ancient national churches will survive in Europe and especially in the United States. But while globalization in the West and North means more religious plurality, the same forces of globalization are making the Middle East less plural and mainly uniformly Muslim. This may mean that the bridging role of the Oriental national churches may cease to exist and the crucial role of Christians in revitalizing the Middle East will be lost forever. In spite of the powerful forces of globalization, the Middle East may again, in the near future, lay in a remote and irrelevant corner of the world.

A theological Reflection

Taking this historical perspective into consideration, allow me to reflect briefly on "Christianity and religious plurality" from a Middle Eastern contextual theological perspective. For it is by a "reflective, witnessing, and living faith" and "faith alone" that a Christian can encounter, interact, live in and contribute to a world of religious plurality. In brief I would like to highlight the following elements of such a "reflective, witnessing and living faith." In doing so, I have Islam in mind, but also Judaism, since the Jewish people and the State of Israel are shaping modern history in the Middle East to a marked degree.

The Messiah Complex

Christians in the Middle East continue to confess that Jesus Christ is the Messiah. The Middle East is currently suffering under several messiah complexes. Many people are still waiting for a new Salahiddin, a new Samson, or even a new Constantine; for a religious, political or economic messiah to come down from heaven, or to rise up from amongst them. As Christians we continue to confess that our Messiah arrived a long time ago. In a context where people are used to solutions either coming from heaven and transforming everything, making all new, or in a context where people expect a prince will appear riding on a white horse to fulfill their dreams, it is essential to confess that we do not need to wait any longer. Heaven has already spoken its Word. The miracle is done. The Gospel of Jesus Christ is the miracle; the power which is transforming people from being spectators in history, to being actors-empowered and liberated. Our salvation is finished, accomplished by grace alone.

We do not need to achieve our own salvation by our deeds, clothing, rituals or even works. In a context of booming Jewish, Muslim or even Christian fundamentalism, we need to confess this fresh, liberating, and relaxing faith that says salvation is complete. Without the burden and worry about our salvation, we can dedicate ourselves to building a community of social justice. As we continue to build an inclusive Middle Eastern society, we still hold to the confession that the Kingdom of God does not come by watching but is already here and near(Luke 17).

Communication

In a global context of religious plurality and mass media, many think that it is a given for diverse religions, nations and cultures to understand each other. The fact that more and more people are using one language does not guarantee that they understand each other. Babel, a Middle Eastern city, is the best example of an ancient imperial capital. Mass media in the 21st century covers crucial events simultaneously across the planet but that does not necessarily mean that people grasp what is happening better or understand each other better. This was never as clear to me as in the last months of the war on Iraq(2003). The one and same war was covered by mainline Arab and American media very differently. For one it was "Operation Iraqi Freedom," for the other "Occupation Iraqi Soil and Oil." Watching an event unfold on TV or computer screens "one can see and yet not see," and "can hear and yet not hear." Breaking news can leave hearts untouched, closed and cold. Having so many mass media options in the global media does not in itself imply that the masses communicate with each other. Providing global news is itself not an added value because those means are never neutral. News agencies are dependent on who owns, runs them, and hears them. They are not good in and of themselves. True communication between peoples and cultures in a global setting is, therefore, never something to take for granted. When real communication in an international setting occurs, it is a miracle, a miracle of the Holy Spirit. Another Middle Eastern city, Jerusalem, became the biblical symbol of this reality on Pentecost where representatives of the whole ancient global community gathered. They spoke in many languages, yet the real miracle was hearing, not speaking; it was a miracle of listening and understanding. This true communication is not a given, but a gift, and it is by grace and grace alone. It is God who gave us Christians in the Middle East, at several points in our history, this gift of understanding. As an integral part of the Arab world we understand how and why our region is as it is, and as part of a worldwide Christian community we understand how and why that other world is as it is. We share values and feelings of both civilizations, and it hurts us to see the gap between those civilizations growing, or to hear theories on the clash of civilizations. We suffer from so many misunderstandings between those two worlds with the larger world. Yet our calling is not just to cry, although we often do. Rather, our historical calling is to translate, to facilitate, to bridge, to help communicate and to share the gift granted to us in Jerusalem at Pentecost.

The Neighbor

Christians in the Middle East continue to address the old/new question: "Who is my neighbor?"At a time when the Middle East is becoming increasingly fragmented into conflicting sub-cultures, where identity is linked to narrow boundaries, to walls erected to separate peoples, and in a context where a neighbor is only one who belongs to the same sect, ideology, nationality or gender(Sunni versus Shiite; Christian versus Muslim; Syrian versus Lebanese, etc...) it is essential to dare to proclaim the "Samaritan" as the potential neighbor. Our region has, historically speaking, been affected by multitudinous conflicts. Because of its diversity, the region has unfortunately never been capable on its own of finding its unity in diversity. Sarcastically speaking, only invading foreign superpowers were able to unite the region under one power, and they were also the ones who divided to rule. For hundreds of years, tribes, nations, religions, cultures and national movements thought of themselves exclusively. For centuries the peoples of the Middle East were busy pushing the neighbor to become the enemy. It is time now to think of transforming the enemy into a neighbor. As Christians we continue to confess that people who cannot think of loving their enemies will soon start hating themselves, that people who are not courageous enough to cross boundaries, will find themselves prisoners in their own constructed ghettos, and that those who cannot show mercy to their opponents will wake one day to see violence penetrating their own homes. We need to work on an inclusive identity; we need to work on the integration of different groups and sub-groups in our society, never losing hope, yet realizing while the process is long and difficult, it is rewarding.

The power in the powerlessness

Christians in the Middle East "continue to proclaim Christ crucified a stumbling block to Jews and foolishness to Gentiles, but to those who are the called, Jews and Greeks, Christ the power of God and the wisdom of God"(1 Cor 1). The issue of power is crucial in the Middle East. Historically, Muslims early on were used to holding the reins of power in Medina. Their confession of "Alahu Akbar"(God is greater) from the Middle Ages to the present seems to be confirmed for the most part by their political, military and economic expansion. Muslims developed a legal system that made them accustomed to being the ruling majority. One of the dilemmas facing Muslims today, however, is to reflect on how it is possible to proclaim the power of God "Alahu Akbar" while globally Muslims are on the loosing end and deprived of power; and how to proclaim the one God while they are so divided. Byzantine Christians in the Middle East were granted political power for only three centuries, while all other Christians were always deprived of power. Lebanon is the sole example in the modern history of the Middle East of Christians being in a majority situation for a time. The norm is that Christians live as a minority. Jews, who were for centuries also deprived of power, had the chance in the 20th century to establish a state where Jews would constitute a majority. Christians, Muslims and Jews were given several different opportunities to hold power. All of them knew first hand what it means to be deprived of power. The challenge for each group was in what to trust more - the power of culture or the culture of power. Holding to power and trusting in it led and is still leading to a culture of violence. In a context where to multiply is seen as something positive, quantity is what matters. And where the voice of the masses is heard, the temptation is great to trust in this culture of power. Being deprived of power taught minorities to trust in the power of culture. As people of faith we have to reflect on this culture of power and violence which is found in most of our religious writings as well as in our political practices. It is always easy to see this culture of power in other religions. It is not easy to admit that it exists in one's own tradition. For frightened Christians in the catacombs making the sign of the cross on their bodies was a sign of faith in the crucified Lord. But for Byzantine soldiers to engrave the cross on their helmets was a sign of a triumphant ideology. Wasn't this the experience of many in the U.S. too on 9/11 when the twin towers fell and the country became so vulnerable? Many then experienced something of the power of the Resurrection as well as the solidarity of the world. What a difference to the context now. When we strive to dominate and when we think we are powerful and that we will prevail, we stumble and become foolish. Our confession remains that the power of God can't be found outside the Cross. Reflecting on this reality is not just a mere academic endeavor, but an urgent call to repentance. Religious plurality does not function without a culture of true repentance. God continues to raise prophetic voices within our diverse cultures, calling each of our communities to true repentance. These prophets are largely witnesses to their own people and sometimes to other peoples. True repentance leads power holders to share their power, and leads the powerless to empowerment. Sharing power and empowerment are two sides of the same coin, and constitute one of the bigger challenges in the Middle East today.

2.

Christianity in the Arabian Peninsula from the End of the Sixth to the Seventh Century

The Arabian Peninsula, the homeland of the Prophet Muhammad, was laying in a quiet and remote corner of the world until the first quarter of the seventh century.[1] Historical events occurred far from the region and it appeared as if the Arabs were condemned to be spectators of history rather than participants. This was due to several factors, the most important of which was that the whole region was in a state of social, political and religious transition. It is in the light of these developments that it is important to look at the rise of Islam.

The Political Context

At the end of the sixth century and the beginning of the seventh, the Arabian Peninsula was remote and distanced from the two great regional powers, the Byzantine Empire in the northwest and the newly-established Persian Empire in the northeast. The Byzantine Empire occupied North Africa, the areas around the Nile, the Sinai Peninsula, Palestine, Syria, Asia Minor and some parts of Europe.
The Persian Empire controlled the area between the Caspian Sea and the Persian Gulf, from the Tigris River in the west to the Oxus and Indus rivers to the east. Its capital was Seleucia Ctesiphon. The borders of the two states met in Mesopotamia in the north of the Arabian

Peninsula, which prompted the two powers to create a buffer zone between the empires. Two Arab tribes who were loyal to one of these two empires inhabited this buffer zone. The Ghassanids[2] were located in the west that is, in the part controlled by the Byzantines. The Lakhmids, by contrast, were in the east within the Persian sphere of influence. The two great major powers did not allow these two tribes to play an influential role in the politics of the region except to safeguard the interests of the states in the region and to act as a buffer. The Arab tribes also had to repel invasions by Bedouin tribes and to protect trade routes. Both powers sought to broaden their spheres of influence in the Arabian Peninsula. This reality influenced the life of Muhammad from the time of his birth until his death.

In the same year that Muhammad was born, Abraha[4] attempted to conquer the Arabian Peninsula from the south. Abraha was an Abyssinian(Ethiopian) and the Viceroy of Yemen, which was under Ethiopian control at that time. Geographically, the Ethiopians were allied with the Byzantines. Abraha's attack was an attempt to block Persian influence in the Arabian Peninsula. Stories tell us that Abraha led his army on an elephant which is why that year was called "The Year of the Elephant." Abraha's military campaign reached the gates of Mecca but ultimately failed because of the spread of pestilence. Abraha himself died shortly after reaching Mecca. The dream of the Byzantines to indirectly control the Arabian Peninsula thus ended. The Persians, however, were more successful. In 572 they attacked the western side of the Persian Gulf from the northeast and parts of the southern Arabian Peninsula, expelling the Ethiopians from the region and gaining direct control.

The second event of political significance occurred in 610[5], the same year of the call of the Prophet Muhammad. Phocas, a Byzantine, usurped the Empire and killed the Emperor Maurice. The Persian King, Khusrau II Parvez, launched a campaign against the

Byzantine Empire and in five years succeeded in occupying eastern Asia Minor, reaching to Chalcedon. The Persian armies came from the north under General Shahin and overran Syria and Palestine in 611, occupying Jerusalem in 614. They then seized Egypt from the Byzantines in 619. In that military campaign, the Persians destroyed thousands of churches and monasteries. They also seized the Holy Cross of Christ in Jerusalem and took it with them. During this period drastic changes occurred in Constantinople. Heraclius(Hercules) arrived with his army and entered the city on October 2, 610, deposed Phocas, and assumed the throne of the Empire. In 621 he launched a counter attack against the Persians and recovered Egypt, Palestine and Syria. He was able to destroy the Persian army with the help of Armenians, Georgians and Khazar in a battle near Nineveh, which led to the destruction of the Persian capital of Seleucia Ctesiphon. Two years after this battle, Heraclius was able to restore Christ's Holy Cross to Jerusalem in a glorious victory procession. But the Byzantines' triumph did not last long. The Persian and Byzantine Empires were weak and exhausted from their wars against each other and at this time a new great power began to emerge in the Arabian Peninsula.

The emergence of a new power took the two great empires by surprise and soon, of necessity, they had to make way for this strong new force. The position of the Arabs vis-á-vis history was no longer one of spectator. Rather, they began to play a main role in regional events. By 630, an army under the leadership of the Prophet Muhammad had subjugated the Arabian Peninsula. The Prophet, however, did not live to witness his followers' conquest of Palestine and Mesopotamia, which occurred during the six years that followed his death. Neither the political background of the two empires nor the role that was made available to the Arabs at the beginning of the seventh century were hidden from the Prophet Muhammad. Qur'anic evidence points to the awareness of these regional events. One example is a Surah from the first Meccan epoch, Surah 105, which is also called

"Surat Al-Feel"(The Elephant). It describes the march of Abraha Al-Ashram to Mecca, the birthplace of the Prophet, attributing his defeat to divine providence that protected this Arab city from harm. According to the Surah, God Himself fought for the protection of the city.

It is worth noting that the call of the Prophet came at a time of political turmoil and political change, as was also true of many prophets in the Old Testament. At the time of his call, Muhammad was a commercial trader. His passage through influential areas in the Persian and Byzantine Empires during business trips was not unlikely; even if those travels did not take place it would have been impossible for one to live in Mecca, a city situated on the most important trade routes of the day, without being influenced by the prevailing political atmosphere. Mecca was believed to have been kept divinely safe from the surrounding political turmoil allowing its trade to prosper. Mecca's success indicates divine providence because God "gave them(Quraysh) food during hunger and gave them security during fear"(Sural Quraysh 106, and also Surat Al-Inshirah 95, 2).

The turmoil around the year 610 was of a revolutionary nature and caused drastic changes in the region. Unsurprisingly, therefore, apocalyptic notions of the end of the world and the Final Judgment played an important role in the early Surahs. According to Noldeke[7] there are forty eight Surahs that date to the early Meccan epoch, twenty of which include direct references and thirteen references to the end of the world. The military events that took place to the north of the Arabian Peninsula suggested that the world was about to perish. The names of some of these Surahs bear witness to that fear:

- Surat al-Layl(Night) number 92
- Surat al-Qari'at(The Striking) number 101
- Surat, al -Zilzal(The Earthquake) number 99
- Surat, al – Infitar(The Cleaving Asunder) number 82

- Surat Kuwirat(The Folding Up) number 81
- Surat al-Inshiqaq(The Rending Asunder) number 84
- Suraat al-Qiyamah(The Resurrection) number 75
- Suraat al-Haqqah(The Infallible) number 69
- Suraat al-Waqi'aa(The Inevitable) numbers 56

Muhammad was confident about the message given to him in the face of these perceived and real calamities and he was able to stir the passions of people and bring them together. He first addressed the inhabitants of his own city, Mecca, and his kinsfolk. In these recitations about the Judgment Day, various images were used, especially Christian images, because eschatology was one of the distinguishing characteristics of the Nestorian Church.[8] It is possible that Christian sermons about the Judgment Day were also heard in the Arabian Peninsula.[9] We have no evidence, however, of any sermons directed to the people of Mecca. Muhammad believed that he was the apostle of the city and did not start to spread his call outside the boundaries of Mecca until later.

Muhammad also did not refer to disputes between the Byzantine and Persian Empires, except in Surah 30, which Noldeke ascribes to the third Meccan epoch. The name of this Surah is "Al-Roum"(the Greeks) and it was received after the fall of Palestine in 614.[10] Verses 2 through 4 of this Surah say, "The Greeks have been overcome by the Persians in the nearest part of the land; but after their defeat, they shall overcome the others in their turn, within a few years. Unto God belongs the disposal of this matter, both for what is past and for what is to come. And on that day(that is when the Byzantines win) the believers shall rejoice in the success granted by God." In these verses, recited by the Prophet, the Byzantines are favored against the Persians. It was expected that the former would defeat the latter, which is what happened. At this point, considered the second Meccan period, Muhammad's position was clearly and unequivocally with the Byzantines because the victory of the Byzantines was the victory of the believers at that time.

The Ecclesiastical Context

As political conditions at the end of the sixth century and the beginning of the seventh century were tumultuous so too was the ecclesiastical context experiencing change. Many contemporary scholars of Christianity at the time of Muhammad portray Christian creeds and Church structure, its rituals, and acts of piety as if they were fully developed. In fact, this was not the case. A great deal of what is related to Christianity in this region was in a state of development; much was not formed and many details had yet to be finalized.

The concept of a "national religion" was one of the key characteristics of the religions of the Fertile Crescent, and to some extent, was the defining element of national identity. This is an often overlooked fact. It is essential, however, to consider the role of religion and identity to understand the impact of the Qur'an on the region. The concept of a national religion means that a people, its civilization, language, identity, and its religion form an inseparable bond in a group's identity. Nationality and religion were thus completely intertwined. Nationality was not the same as its modern meaning denotes a concept which was developed in the 18th and 19th centuries. Rather, this earlier definition of religion and nationality applies to the three religions with which Muhammad became familiar. Zoroastrianism(from Zoroaster) was the religion of the Persian Empire and was closely connected to Persian identity and the Persian language. The same is true for Judaism, although the Jews had no geographical region of their own at the time of Muhammad. Nevertheless, Judaism was a national religion because the people and their religion were strongly intertwined. Jewish religious rituals in Arab regions used Hebrew. Tradition says that Judaism was a national religion with its own region in the southwest of the Arabian Peninsula. This tradition may be traced to Dhu Nuwas, King of Himyar, who embraced Judaism between 522-525, CE. It is generally assumed that Christianity did not follow this model of national identity because from the beginning Christianity was committed to a missionary vision and was not connected with any particular language or people. This is in accordance with Jesus' command, "Go and make disciples of all nations"(Matthew 28:16-20). Although Christianity was not national but rather international in nature its ecclesiastical makeup had a national hue from the start. National churches grew whose members were closely tied to different cultures and languages. This fusion of faith and nationality was extremely important for churches to connect religion to their contexts, as shown below.

The Melkite Church

This name symbolizes the church of the Byzantine Empire, which supported the Chalcedon Council in 451. The name "Melkite" was not its original name rather it is derived from the word "malka" in Syriac and "malek" in Arabic. Melkite was a nickname given to the church by the non-Chalcedonian Christians in the 10th century, alluding to the belief that the Chalcedonians in that Council did not follow pure Christian teaching but submitted to the authority of Caesar Marcion. The state and the Melkite Church were closely intermeshed. At the end of the sixth century and the beginning of the seventh, the Melkite Church was the official church of the Byzantine Empire and had three patriarchs; the Patriarch of Alexandria, the Patriarch of Antioch, and the Patriarch of Jerusalem. Culturally, the Melkite Church was characterized by its purely Greek hue because its followers were either Greeks or non-Greeks of the educated class who had adopted Greek culture and were Hellenized. The church could not include in its membership a large number of citizens who spoke Syriac; the inhabitants of villages, desert and mountainous areas in Syria, Palestine, and Egypt. The language of the Melkite Church was thus the language of its culture, Greek. Greek was also the language of their Bible and of their religious rituals. The Prophet Muhammad was familiar with Byzantine matters as indicated by the aforementioned verses, and his support of the Byzantines was connected to the devoutness of their faith.

The Nestorian Church[11]

This name refers to the church that settled in the areas of Mesopotamia included in the Persian Empire. Although the church bore the name of Nestorius, whose teachings were rejected and condemned at the Council of Ephesus in 431, it declared that it was the successor of the Seat of Antioch and that it was the mother of all patriarchates.[12] As a result of the conflicts between the Byzantines and the Persians, the Christians living around the Tigris and Euphrates rivers were gradually forced away from the Byzantines in order to preserve their identity in the region. They declared their autonomy at the first administrative Council of Seleucia Ctesiphon, held in the capital of the Persian Empire in 410. They also declared that their church had become a national and independent church in 424. From that time, it was headed by a special leader called "Catholicus." The church was divided into several bishoprics and centers of archbishops. Not long after the division of creeds took place and the teachings of Nestorius were condemned at the Council of Ephesus in 431. By this condemnation, the Nestorian Church was not only divided politically from the church in Byzantium but also divided dogmatically. In addition, the church's separation from the Byzantine Empire was cultural. Cultural differences played a significant role in the formation of creeds as well. From a cultural standpoint, the Nestorians considered themselves to be successors of the Assyrians.

Their language was not Greek but eastern Syriac, the language into which the Bible had been translated early on.[13] It was also the language of the church's liturgy and religious rites. The Nestorian Church, which is today called the Assyrian Church, was one of the most prosperous churches in the east. Almost from its beginning its missionary work spread in the Persian Gulf up to the south of the Arabian Peninsula. In the middle of the third century there was a special bishop for Qatar and Bahrain. After the Persians occupied the Arabian Peninsula, information about the Nestorian bishoprics in Sanaa', the Island of Socotra, and in Yemen began to emerge. Nestorian bishoprics were established in Syria and Palestine too at the beginning of the seventh century after the Persian occupation in 614.

In the fourth century, Nestorian missionaries arrived in southwest India and were in China by 635. The missionaries naturally followed the trade routes of the Silk Road and it is possible that they had contact with Mecca as a commercial city on the trade route. One can assume that the Prophet Muhammad was also acquainted with the Nestorians, especially as he was a merchant.

The Monophysite National Churches

Like the political and cultural factors that called for establishing a special Assyrian national church, there were also theological and cultural reasons that created three other national churches. The reason for establishing these churches was connected to the debates on the person of Christ, which took place at the Council of Chalcedon in 451. The formula ratified by the Council stated that there are two natures of Christ that do not accept "integration or separation." This is the formula that Caesar Marcion wanted to impose forcefully in order to preserve the unity of his empire. The Greeks and the Romans accepted this formula but the Christians in the east opposed it. These eastern Christians became known as "Monophysites" because they saw in the Word Incarnate one nature only: divine-human. These churches are divided into three categories with their own distinctive cultural characteristics. They are:

The Armenian Church

This church traces its origins to the disciple Bartholomew and the apostle Thaddeus. Armenia was Christianized by Gregory the Enlightened who died in 325 during the reign of King Terridates III(252-330). Accordingly, Armenia was partitioned between the Byzantine and Persian Empires in 387. Because its bishops were ordained in Caesarea Cappadocia(south of the Black Sea), on Byzantine territory, the church adopted the resolutions of Chalcedon. These teachings were refuted at the Council of Vagharshapat, after contact was established with the Jacobite Church. Chalcedonian teachings were again refuted at the Council of Dvin in 527. Among the national churches, there was no church like the Armenian Church, which played its national role with great splendor. The Armenian people and their religion are an inseparable unit. As well, the Armenians have their own language, an Indo-European tongue developed by Ma'roub at the beginning of the fifth century. Armenia's geographical position allowed for the inclusion of Persian, Greek, and Syriac linguistic influences. Soon Scripture, ecclesiastical rituals, and Christian writings were translated into this new language.[14] The location of this church, to the southeast of the Black Sea and its vast distance from the Arabian

Peninsula, allows one to assume that Muhammad was not aware of this church nor did he have contact with any of its members.

The Jacobite Church

The Jacobite National Syrian Church is found mostly[15] on Byzantine land, particularly in the mountainous areas of Syria and Palestine as well as in Asia Minor and Mesopotamia. The vast majority of its followers are from the region of present day Syria. Antioch was the center for these Christians until the Melkites expelled them at the beginning of the sixth century. The Syrians openly opposed Chalcedonian resolutions and differed with the Byzantines. Jacob Baradeus is credited with organizing these Christians and thus the church is named after him. Jacob's success in unifying the Christians in Syria was possible with the help of two people, the prince of the Ghassanids, Al-Harith Ibn Jabala, and Czarina Theodora. Al-Harith Ibn Jabala approached the Czarina in 453 and requested her approval to ordain Baradeus, Bishop for Edessa(Al-Raha). Czarina Theodora, wife of Czar Justinian, was of Monophysite origin. She was known for her protection of the Monophysites and permitting integration into the Byzantine Empire; facts not concealed from her husband. Indeed, she had the Monophysite Alexandrian Patriarch, who was under her protection, perform the ordination service. Two other Syrian monks were also ordained bishops with support from Constantinople. This allowed Baradeus and the two bishops to travel in the east, ordain priests, and organize the affairs of denominations. Thus the Syrian Church grew and spread in the Byzantine Empire in the middle of the sixth century. The language of this church was a western Syriac tongue into which the Bible had earlier on been translated. The translation was called "Tergum Bishita." A liturgy grew in Edessa(later known as Al-Raha) and canticles for the church were organized. Another important characteristic of the Syrian Church was its monastic organization. Unlike monasteries in the West, monks in the East were restricted to being hermits and ascetics who abandoned the world and went into the desert, to remote mountains, and to arid plains to spend their lives in prayer and completely renounce the world. The deserts of Palestine, Sinai, Jordan, and Syria were full of such monks. Muhammad knew of these monks and the Qur'an itself emphasized monasticism. There were no disputes between Muhammad and the monastic system until later in the Medinan epoch[16]. The position of the Qur'an concerning the monasteries thus vacillated between praise on the one hand and reformative criticism on the other. [17]

The Coptic National Church

This church and the Syrian monophysite church share several characteristics. The Coptic Church, however, is based on Egyptian soil and ascribes its establishment to the Evangelist Mark. Alexandria was one of the most important centers of church theology in ancient times and later it was elevated to one of the early patriarchate seats. Monks and monasteries in Egypt played key roles in church history of the Nile region. The Christians of Egypt rejected the resolutions of the Council of Ephesus in 431 and from that time, the Copts and western Syrians have been allied against the Melkites. One Syrian monk named Damian, who lived between 578-605, helped the Copts establish their national church. These Christians also had a unique national identity that began with the Pharaohs. There were many local Coptic dialects among the inhabitants of Egypt. The Septuagint was translated into Coptic in the third or fourth century. While the Coptic language was declared the official language of the church and its rituals, [18] intellectuals also used Greek.

Although Egypt is somewhat distant from Mecca it is known that there was a relationship between Muhammad and the Copts. One example of this connection is the prophet's wife Maria, an Egyptian female slave who was given to the Prophet by the Byzantine-appointed governor of Egypt in 627-629. Maria gave birth to his only son, Ibrahim, who died shortly afterwards in 632[19]. The relationship of the Prophet to the Copts most likely took place shortly before his death. Yet Islamic literature suggests that this relationship might also have taken place before the Prophet's call to Islam.[20]

The Ethiopian Church

The church in Ethiopia followed Alexandria and traces its establishment back to the Treasurer, Queen Kindaka's Minister of Finance. Christianity entered Ethiopia through Fromantius and Aesius. The church was declared the official church in the reign of King Izna in the Kingdom of Axome, around 320-342. One of its first bishops was Fromantius, who was ordained a bishop by Patriarch Athanasius in 330. This ordination established a bond between the Ethiopian and the Coptic Churches. From early on there was a connection between Axome and the Syrian Monophysite doctrines because the Jacobite monks introduced teachings that opposed Chalcedon around the year 480. They also introduced Syrian rituals and customs in addition to translating the scriptures into the language of Ge-ez.[21] Egypt declared the Coptic language of Ge-ez as its official and sole language. The language of Ge-ez thus became a religious and holy language because Scripture was translated into this local language between 677-678.[22]

The Prophet had a great deal of contact with Ethiopian Christians.[23] It is worthwhile noting Bilal, an Ethiopian slave, who is described by Islamic tradition as one of the first followers of Muhammad and among his most sincere adherents. Tradition says that the nurse of the Prophet, Umm Ayman, was also an Ethiopian. The Prophet was in contact with another Ethiopian slave too named Jaber, who is described as loudly reciting verses from the Torah and the Gospel. Some Muslim historians describe the Prophet as knowing the Abyssinian language. It is certain that the Qur'an contains about two hundred words borrowed from Ge-ez. When the Prophet was in great distress in Mecca in 615, he sent most of his followers to Christian Ethiopia. They were, according to tradition eighty nine men and eighteen women. The Prophet's decision to send his followers to take refuge in a Christian kingdom is of special significance. Islamic tradition states that the Meccan refugees recited verses from Surat Mariam in front of King Al-Najashi[24] and Bishop Fersi. It is understood that they wanted to show Islam as a form of Christianity.

In summation, Christians around the Arabian Peninsula established national churches in which faith became intertwined with culture, language, and local national identity. These components of identity-became enmeshed, as was also the case with the Jews and the Zoroastrians. In spite of this, the development of Eastern Christianity into national churches should not be considered final because many things were still in a state of flux, even in the sixth and seventh centuries. In the seventh century, a new national church emerged in the mountains of Lebanon, known as the Maronite Church. This church was established over theological controversies about the interpretation of the person of Christ, that is, about monergism and monotheletism. Theological interpretations had not evolved formally and definitely even in the seventh century. For this reason; if we judge Islam only in light of Nicea and Ephesus, our creedal conclusions are anachronistic.

Most of these national churches were located around the Arabian Peninsula and some of the Peninsula inhabitants belonged to these churches.

There were also Arab Christian tribes.[25] These tribes can be divided into three different categories:

The Ghassanids [26]

An Arabian dynasty of Yemenite origin, the Ghassanids settled in a region under Byzantine rule, extending from Petra in the south to Syria and Palmyra in the north and Basra and the Euphrates to the east. The Ghassanids reached the zenith of their glory in the second and third quarters of the sixth century when they succeeded in unifying the various Arab tribes who lived in the region. Although their territory was located within the Byzantine Empire, their creed was that of the Monophysites, which in many instances enabled them to act as intermediaries. As mentioned earlier, the Syrian Jacobite Church was indebted to the Ghassanids for its existence because of their patriarch, Al-Harith.[27] Al-Harith made the ordination of Jacob Baradeus and Theodoros, as bishops, in 542 possible, with the support of Czarina Theodora. The Patriarch of Alexandria performed the ordination. While Baradeus attended mainly to the city of Edessa(later Al-Raha), Theodoros, according to Syrian sources, was bishop of the desert, responsible for the Arabian and Bedouin tribes who lived in the areas of Houran. In 563, Jacob Baradeus sent Al-Harith on a mission to Constantinople to be his deputy in the controversy over the heretical creed of three godheads:(the Father, the Son, and the Holy Spirit as three separate and distinct gods). The Monophysite position of the Gassanids, however, led to the downfall of their state. Everything that had been achieved in the reign of Justinian I(518-536) could not be preserved or expanded upon in the reign of Tiberius(582-602). Tiberius arrested the successors of Al-Harith and later deported them breaking the unity of the tribes. The Ghassanids continued to live their tribal life but they did not witness a second age of prosperity. Although Caliph Umar occupied their region they remained faithful to Christianity. Culturally, the Ghassanids were Arabs and their language was Arabic. No national church, however, was established. They thus maintained a dependent relationship with the Syrian "mother church." In short, priesthood, religious rites, and the scriptures were not Arabized but remained in Syriac.

The Lakhmids or Al-Manathera

These people originated from the middle of the Arabian Peninsula and settled in the middle of Mesepotamia(Beit Arbaya) and Babylon. Their nexus was Al-Hira. Unlike the Gassanids, the majority were craftsmen or urban traders who lived in cities. The Lakhmid kings generally were not Christians, but showed religious tolerance to their subjects. The relationship between the Lakhmids and the Byzantines was pronounced because their region was within the Persian sphere of influence and they were also strongly influenced by the Nestorian doctrine. The bishop of Al-Hira Hosha' attended the Council of Seleucia Ctesiphon, which legally established the Nestorian constitutional system. The Council of Merkabta, which took place in Lakhmid territory in 420, ratified their administrative separation from Antioch. The City of Merkabta was also in Lakhmid territory. It is certain that their leader, King Nu'man IV, did not embrace the Nestorian creed before the year 592. Lakhmid rule was, however not destined to last beyond the beginning of the seventh century. The Lakhmids were Arab in culture, which is confirmed by the great number of Arab Christian poets who became prominent among the Lakhmids.[29] Ecclesiastically, the Lakhmids continued their dependent relationship with the Nestorian "mother church." They too did not establish an Arab national church and the language of their religious church remained Syriac. Yet one cannot help admiring, the splendor of Lakhmid Arabic poetry.[30]

The Christians of Najran

The third center for Christians in the Arabian Peninsula was in the southwest. Christianity entered the region in the middle of the second century via merchants who passed along the trade routes. The first Christians in this region were thus not Arabs, but were Greeks, Ethiopians or Syrians.[31] As for the original Arab inhabitants, they were not pagans but Arab monotheists whose faith can be traced to Abraham and his wife Qatoura.[32]

Najran was the center of Christianity in the southwest of the Arabian Peninsula a fertile valley that was situated at the crossroads of two trade routes, one leading to the Mediterranean in the north and the other to Iraq in the east. There are many legends that tell about the coming of Christianity to Najran. Several Christian sects were found in Najran at the beginning of the sixth century. Dhu Nuwas, who embraced Judaism, invaded Najaran and forced the Christians to renounce their faith or be killed. Many preferred to die rather than to betray their faith thus becoming martyrs. Records indicate that a large number of these martyrs were Arabs. The mystics and clergy, however, were not Arabs. Among the martyrs were two priests, Moses and Elia, whose origins are Al-Hira; the priest Sergius, and the deacon Hanania whose origin is Rumi or Greece; the priest Abraham the Persian, who was perhaps Syrian; and the deacon Yunan, who was Abyssinian. The list of martyrs also included Arabic names, which were typically from the south.[33]

Najran returned to Christian control in the year 525 after the Ethiopians invaded and killed Dhu Nuwas. Najran became a holy city for Arab Christians in the south of the Arabian Peninsula and its monastery a place of Christian pilgrimage. It was a refuge to which the persecuted flocked as told by the poets who sang its praises.[34]

It is possible to confirm historically that Muhammad was knowledgeable about the Christians of Najran. But the relation between "The People of the Trench" which is mentioned in Surat Al-Burouj(85:4-9) and the martyrs of Najran[35] is not certain. The text, says: "May the people of the trench be killed(that is, a curse is on them), the fire be fueled(the fire of hell the fuel of which is not finished), as they sit on it(that is, on the fire of hell on the Day of Reckoning), and they are witnesses to what they do(what they did during their lives to believers), and how they avenged them except that they believe in the Mighty and Praiseworthy God(that is, what they transferred from the believers) who has the kingdom of Heavens and earth, and God is the witness of everything."

If these verses are a depiction of Najran martyrdom, they provide further evidence that Muhammad had close ties with the Christians of Najran. It is known that the Prophet met with the Christians of Najran during the period of Al-Wufoud, in 628, in which an agreement was made in a letter of covenant. The text states: "The apostle of God wrote to the bishops of Najran, their priests, followers and monks... that the people of Najran and its followers enjoy the protection of God and the safeguard of his Apostle. There is a guarantee of protection for them, their society, their land, their property, their churches, and the practicing of their rites. Neither the church leaders nor the loyals(who give and take rights) will be forced to leave their positions. There is a guarantee of protection for whomever is on their land, small or big, provided that their wealth did not come from usury or blood money[36](what hired murderers receive in the pagan times)." From that time on the relationship of the Prophet towards Christians began to change. He would adopt a new attitude after the Medinan epoch.

In summary, Christians outside the Arabian Peninsula established national churches while Christians in the Arabian

Peninsula did not; remaining mostly dependent on their "mother church" in matters related to clergy, religious rituals, and ecclesiastic language. This fact is peculiar since missionaries of national churches in the east made it a priority to translate the Bible into local languages. Even when they were not able to translate the entire Bible, they managed at least to translate those portions related to liturgy. These missionaries became the force behind establishing national Christian literature.[37] The scholar Baumstark compares this phenomenon with the context of the Arabian Peninsula and argues that taking the above into consideration it is not possible to ascertain if religious texts in the Arabic language existed for Arab Christians in the Arabian Peninsula until the seventh century.[38]

The question of the existence of Arab Christian literature before pre-Islamic times is highly disputed. The reasons for this are due both to an emotional attachment to the issue and to contradictory evidence. Those who believe in the existence of such writings are either Arab Christians, for whom it is important to discover their Arab Christian heritage before Islam,[39] or Orientalists who want to confirm the relationship between the Qur'an and the Bible.[40] Scholars who deny the existence of these writings wish to show that Christianity among the Arabs has not been established, its origin cannot be traced,[41] and that pre-Islamic Arabs did not have a Christian faith based on the Bible. It is believed that this non-Biblical form of Christianity caused misunderstandings for Muhammad[42] concerning the Trinity(the Father, the Son, and Mary) and other elements of Christianity.

It is my opinion that the existence of distinct Arabic Christian literature before Islam is a remote possibility because of the political and cultural situation during the sixth and seventh centuries; namely that Arab Christians did not have an absolute national identity. This lack of identity explains the almost continuous state of war between the Ghassanids and the Lakhmids, two Arab Christian tribes. The other reason for the state of chronic fighting between them was that both tribes were not politically independent. This incompleteness also applies to the Church. Christian Arab tribes were dispersed into sects and belonged to three different doctrines: the Nestorian(the Lakhmids), the Syrian Monophysite(The Ghassanids), and the Ethiopian(Najran). While the national factor and doctrinal factors played important roles with national churches in their struggle for political and religious autonomy, against the Byzantine Empire, these two factors were nonexistent in Arab Christian tribes before Islam.

This fact does not mean that the Christian Arabs were in a state of immobility. On the contrary, there was much activity. The time from the turn of the sixth century to the seventh was characterized as a period of transition and searching. Something was expected because there was such great turmoil and change. Islam, however, prevented these changes from taking place. Indeed Islam arose from this very cauldron and was able to attain its success and completeness from changes in the political situation. The oldest Arabic manuscripts confirm that Arab Christians were in a stage of transition. In fact, the Arabic script in which the Qur'an was written, known as the Kufi script, was developed in Al-Hira by the ᶜAbbadiyyoun.[43] Among the oldest Arabic manuscripts that have been preserved for us, two copies are of Christian origin. They are the Ziad manuscript(southeast of Aleppo) which dates to the year 512, and the Haran manuscript, which can be traced to the year 568. They show that Arab Christians were experiencing a transitional stage because the two manuscripts were not only written in Arabic but also in Greek and Syriac.[44] Although the Bible had not been rendered in Arabic,[45] Christian sermons in Arabic were beginning to appear. One of the most famous Christian preachers before Islam was Qass Bin Saida Al-Ayadi, mentioned earlier. He belonged to the Iyad tribe and was renowned for his poetry and speeches, which were highly eloquent. Al-Ayadi died around the year 600 in Aleppo, according to stories. His first name was Farid, in Arabic, according to etymology possibly derived from "Qass" or Qassis" which is given to a priest or a Christian, religious man. This has led some to speculate that he was the Bishop of Najran. Abu Al-Faraj Al-Asbahani(Ali Bin Al- Husayn), a prominent historian and linguist, conveyed the following story in Kitab Al-Aghani, which he wrote around the middle of the tenth century: "When the delegation of Iyad came to the Prophet, he asked them: "How is Qass Bin Saida?" They replied, "O, Apostle of God, he died." He said, "I can imagine him in front of my eyes in 'Ukaz Market, riding his gray camel and delivering a speech that inflamed the people, but, unfortunately, I do not remember the words." A member of the delegation said: "O, Apostle of God, I remember it." The Prophet asked him, "What are the words of the sermon that you heard?" He replied: "I heard him preaching as follows:

"0, people, hear and understand. Anyone who has lived died, and the one who has died and passed away, and all that is coming, will come. A black night, a quiet day, a sky with horoscopes, twinkling stars, teeming seas, established mountains, a flat land, and running rivers. In the heavens there is news and on the earth there are lessons. Why are people going but not returning? Were they satisfied and stayed there? Or were they left and now sleep? O, people of Iyad, where are the fathers and the grandfathers, and where are the mighty Pharaohs? Were not they wealthier than you and lived longer than you? Time has ground them in his chest and torn them by its audacity. Those who have perished for centuries before us, we can gain insight. When I saw a cause for death that has no source, and I saw my people, the lowly and the great, walking towards death. The past does not return to me as one who has remained. I was certain that it is inevitable. I will go where the people have gone[46]"

One needs to hear this sermon read in a loud voice in Arabic to experience the poetic meter which characterizes its orator.

Listening to this sermon in such a way allows one to easily ascertain its kinship to rhythmical verses in the Qur'an. Qass Bin Sa'ida was the first to create a Christian Arab sermon that incorporates the social and poetical environment in the Arabian Peninsula at that time and express it in a splendid literary format. Qass greatly influenced the Prophet because the Prophet wanted the Arab world to be religiously and politically changed and the soil was receptive to his desire.

3.

Contextualizing the Scripture

Towards a New Understanding of the Qur'an
An Arab Christian Perspective

Introduction

Over the course of history Christian theologians have adopted various approaches to understanding the Qur'an. Throughout the Middle Ages, for example, a polemical method was preponderant among most theologians who simply took the Bible as the "true" scripture and canonical basis from which to develop arguments against the invalidity of the Qur'an. At other times, especially after the Enlightenment, new approaches emerged. These included the historical-critical analysis of scripture; the traditionsgeschichtliche study of the history of scripture in the context of the religious community which professes its holiness; and the literary approach of those who, following the 19th century German scholar, Max Muller, have taken a comparative approach to scripture. In the post World War II era, the studies of Wilfred Cantwell Smith,[1] Heikke Raisanen[2] and Hans Kung[3] have paved the way towards a new understanding of the Qur'an which bears important potential for a new missiological approach.

In this paper I wish to study the Qur'an from the perspective of a contextual Arab theologian, a member of an Arab(Palestinian)

Christian community which has lived within Islamic society for many hundreds of years[4].

Islam has been the most significant component in the world of Arab Christianity for almost 1400 years. Arab Christians and Muslims share Arabic culture, history and language; their fate is intertwined and inseparable. Likewise, Arab Christians are an inseparable part of the world of Islam. Dialogue with Muslims is a necessary and important aspect of Arab Christians' life and survival[5].

The challenge facing Arab Christians is, however, two-fold. Just as Arab Christians are part of the Arab Islamic world, so they are an inseparable part of the Christian world. They belong to both the Arab nation and the universal Church. Belonging to two worlds has, for centuries, constituted a great challenge which is not easy to resolve. Sometimes it appeared as though Arab Christians fell between two chairs. They were often misunderstood and betrayed by both sides . . . But Arab Christians were also able to profit very often from this double belonging . . . they functioned both as transcenders of borders and as bridge builders[6].

It is with bridge building, in relation to the way Christians and Muslims read the Qur'an, that I am concerned in this paper. I write with both Christians and Muslims in mind. As a Christian theologian I am grounded in Christian understandings of revelation and history, and I have been trained in historical as well as theological methods for studying the Bible. My hermeneutical approach to scripture arises from and is an expression of my Christian identity. But my identity as an Arab Christian demands that I approach the Qur'an not as an alien scripture - an alien "other" in competition or conflict with the Bible - but rather as another scripture which has had, and continues to have an immense influence on the moral values and socio-political character of the society to which I fully belong. I recognize that Muslims have their distinctive ways of understanding and interpreting scripture, both the Qur'an and the Bible. Western scholars often stereotype these as pre-critical in contrast to Western critical mythologies. Without being drawn into this debate, I would simply insist that this is an example of the Arab Christian experience of falling between chairs. Rather than foundering in such a quagmire, I shall try to build bridges. In this paper I propose to explore an Arab Christian approach to the Qur'an which may help Western Christians toward a greater appreciation of its scriptural value, and at the same time show Muslims that Christians can engage with their(Muslim) sacred text in a constructive manner. My approach is grounded in my commitment to contextual theology. "The context of Christian Arabs is the Arab-Islamic space"[7]. If the plurality of religions in the Middle East has frequently been exploited for divisive political goals, a priority of contextual theology is to redefine the concept of religion as "a positive relationship between God and humans, simultaneously forming the basis for all of a person's relationships to other human beings and the environment"[8]. The question which therefore faces an Arab Christian contextual theologian is: how to develop a contextual approach to the understanding of Muslim scripture which can provide a basis for Christian-Muslim relationship within contemporary Arab society?

Two methodological principles are involved in answering this question. In search of a renewed understanding of the plurality of religions in Arab culture, it is imperative to deal carefully with history. A Christian contextual approach to the Qur'an will thus take seriously that the Qur'an's original meaning in history always depended on the context of the Prophet Muhammad. Muslims themselves have recognized this from the beginning, and the most creative Muslim experimentation in a modern scriptural hermeneutic - as illustrated for example by Muhammad Arkoun[9] provides convincing evidence that contextual approaches to scripture are by no means foreign to contemporary Islamic scholarship.

A second methodological principle of contextual theology is that it must strive to be a truly local theology. This is where, I maintain, Arab Christians have a qualitative advantage over their Western co-religionists in terms of understanding the Qur'an. The Qur'an identifies itself as "an Arabic Qur'an"[10]. Arabic is a language shared by Muslims and Christians in the Arab world. The Arabic language has deeply influenced the liturgical and theological character of Arab Christianity. It is also the definitive language of Islamic faith and practice. Linguistically and culturally, therefore, the two religious traditions share a common space. From within this space the Qur'an, as will be discussed in the body of this paper, engages contextually with important elements of the biblical tradition: for example, the enculturation of many biblical stories, as well as the contextualization of Jewish-Christian theology and methodology. In a precise sense, which I shall clarify later, the Qur'an may be said in Christian perspective to represent an attempt to arabize the biblical message. To the degree that this is so, it is my conviction that Arab Christianity may, therefore, offer meaningful analogies which, from a Christian perspective, may open the way to a deeper understanding of the Qur'an and of the Prophet Muhammad.

The Qur'an in the first Meccan Period

A Warning to the Meccans

Today, on the basis of the research of the great German scholar of Islam, Theodor Noldeke, it is generally accepted among scholars that the suras(chapters) of the Qur'an can be identified and dated by

Contextualizing the Scripture

the linguistic style of the earliest Meccan suras. As Noldeke wrote: The speech is majestic, rich and full of audacious images; the rhetoric momentum has completely poetic colors. The fervent movement, which is often interrupted by simple yet powerful, gentle information, and the colorful discrepancies are reflected in the short verses, and the whole speech rhymes and consists of a big yet unexpectedly pleasant color[11].

The early Meccan suras are different from those that followed, not only in style, but also in content. Stylistically their form is very similar to that of the ancient Arabian kahin or "soothsayer"[12]. It was on these grounds that Muhammad's critics, seeking to impugn his claim to speak as a prophet, likened him to a poet, an obsessed man or a soothsayer[13]. The content of these early suras also provided grounds for such a comparison. The role of the kahin was always locally bound. The Prophet's emphasis on being sent to a particular tribe, the Banu Hashim[14], as a scion of the tribal confederacy of Quraish[15], and thus to the people of Mecca, over whom the Quraish exercised its hegemony, corresponds to the localism of the Arabian soothsayer.

In these early suras, the single instance of the use of the word qur'an conveys the meaning of "recitation." This denotes the function which Muhammad fulfilled - being commanded by God to "recite" what was revealed to him[16] as distinct from the name of the message which he conveyed. Insofar as the message had a single name, Muhammad typically referred to it as a tadkira or "warning"[17], or amr, "order"[18]. This can be understood within the earliest context of Muhammad's ministry in which he confronted the ubiquitous phenomenon of idol worship among the people of Mecca. His message was one of exhortation to his Meccan kinsfolk to believe in one God, remember God's warnings, and to escape the blazes of hell.

In support of these admonitions, Muhammad reminded his audience that the same message is found in "the writings of Abraham and Moses"[19], whose message was nonetheless valid for Arabs as well. Importantly, however, he added to these the testimony of several non-biblical Arab prophets - Hud[20], Salih[21] and later on Shu'aib [22]. This is critical for understanding Muhammad's Arabian contextuality. From the outset of his preaching, Muhammad integrated Arab prophets into his sermons, showing how they were sent to their people and clans, and how, in contradiction of their preaching, these peoples and clans allowed themselves to be lured back into paganism, for which God punished them. Featuring as keystones of his early message, these stories demonstrate how Muhammad used his Arabian context as the criterion for selecting and utilizing the other traditions - specifically those of Abraham and Moses - from which he drew. The Prophet spoke from within his context, with the result that he offered a thoroughly contextualized rendering of the Abrahamic message.

The Qur'an in the second and third Meccan Periods

Following the development of Muhammad's preaching into the later Meccan periods, which Noldeke identifies, several themes and emphases which amplify the Prophet's sense of contextuality emerged.

A.
Muhammad's self-identification as a prophet for the Arabs

The Meccans resisted Muhammad's message so fiercely that the future of his entire mission was jeopardized. This compelled him to seek an alternative location in which his early followers could mould themselves into a new community. In 615 AD Muhammad sent his followers to Abyssinia in what was to be the first Hijra or "emigration." The only information we have about what actually occurred once the émigrés reached Abyssinia are the stories which have been transmitted in the Islamic tradition. These tell of the Muslim representatives receiving the hospitality of the Abyssinian king(Negus, [Ar.] Najashi), and of friendly conversations which are alleged to have taken place about the sanctity of Jesus and Mary[23]. Although the Qur'an is said to contain certain verses that were revealed to Muhammad in relation to this event[24], the scripture does not contain any historical reference to the event itself. Nor do we have any information from other sources, including - most unfortunately - any of indigenous Abyssinian Christian provenances.

It is not unreasonable to suggest that from this time Muhammad's message underwent a transformation of style and content. As his utterances became more elaborate, it is clear that Muhammad was determined to distance himself from the culture of the kahin with its parochial localism and pagan associations and that he turned more frequently towards other revealed religions. One of the reasons for this was that the Prophet now had a young community which was in search of a communal identity. The question of identity was highlighted by the encounter with Abyssinian Christians. In theological terms this raised the question: was Muhammad's message identical, similar or different from that of the Abyssinian Christians? This then raised the question of the relation between the Bible and Qur'an. The Islamic tradition reveals that Muslim émigrés in Abyssinia recited part of Sura Mariam, the chapter of Mary[25], where the story of the birth of Jesus is reported in order to show that the qur'anic message was in accordance with the biblical one. The conversion of one of Muhammad's followers to Christianity and his decision to stay in Abyssinia had raised awkward questions for the young Islamic community. It was time, therefore, to address the question of Islam's relationships to the other revealed religions.

To employ the terminology of Christian theology, the issue of Heils geschichte had to be addressed. How did Muhammad articulate the unfolding purposes of God in history? How did he understand the relationship between the events in which he was caught up as God's instrument of change and the action of God in and through other revealed religions? A study of the suras belonging to the second and third Meccan periods shows that a simple linear story of "salvation history," progressing in a direct line from beginning to end, did not commend itself to the Prophet. In contrast to this construction of the biblical view, the qur'anic concept presents a "decentralized" interpretation of God's action in the history of human communities.

I prefer the term "decentralized" to the misleading concept of "cyclical" history which the German scholar, Johann Fuck, has suggested[26]. The Heilsgeschichte of the Qur'an does not have a center comparable to the Jewish understanding of the People of Israel and the Christian understanding of Jesus Christ. Qur'anic Heilsgeschichte is decentralized. It was no longer bound exclusively to a Judeo-Christian context but it was, as mentioned, an important place for the Arab prophets none of whom is mentioned in the Bible. The qur'anic Heilsgeschichte underlines that God calls a special prophet from within each "people" (qawm[27]). The prophet is ordained to the task of calling his people, in their language, to turn to God in true monotheistic faith, trusting that God alone is worthy of their worship and obedience[28]. A decentralized Heilsgechichte runs the obvious danger of losing its unity. The Qur'an resolves this problem by insisting that unity lies in the message which prophets preach. Wheresoever God has called them, and among the many different peoples to whom they are sent, prophets are united by the fact that their message comes from the one and only God. What binds the prophets, therefore, is the message itself, which remains universally the same.

A good illustration of this understanding of Heilsgeschichte may be found in Surat Hud[29] which takes its name from one of the Arab prophets -the prophet Hud- who was sent to the people of 'Ad. The first two verses of the chapter provide a clear statement of the prophet understanding of the divine origin of the Qur'an and his specific ministry:

AL R[30] (this is) a book, with verses of which are known and then separated(from each other), from the (One who is) Wise and Instructed(of all), (which teaches) that you should worship, none but God (the only God); truly He sends me to bring you a warning and to announce the good (of previous messages)[31].

The chapter then continues with a summary of the message preached universally by Muhammad and all previous prophets:

"Seek forgiveness from your Lord and direct yourself (repentantly) to Him, and He will grant you over a certain period of time a goodly provision which is favorable to you, to show you His grace. However, if you distance yourself from Him, I fear that punishment will overcome you one great day. Direct yourself to God. He is the Almighty." [32]

Later the story of the Prophet Noah is told, the central tenet of his preaching being expressed in words identical to those cited above:

"We sent Noah (as our messenger) to his people. (He said :) 'I am the one who will warn you clearly, that you must serve none but God. I fear that punishment will overcome you one terrible day." [33]

The chapter then recounts the stories of the non-biblical Arab prophets,

"And then to 'Ad(we sent) their brother Hud (as our messenger)... And to Thamud(we sent) their brother Salih(as our messenger)... And to Madyan(we sent) their brother Shu'aib." [34]

Finally, the chapter turns to the story of Moses who preached the divinely-ordained message of the prophets to Pharoah[35]. In this manner Surat Hud offers an instructive example of the way in which the middle and later Meccan portions of the Qur'an develop a fascinating interplay between the stories of the biblical and extra-biblical prophets in what I have termed a decentralized Heilsgeschichte.[36] The prophets were sent to their peoples with a monotheist message; the message was mostly received with disbelief, except for a faithful few who listened, repented, believed and lived righteously. In contrast to these few, however, the unbelievers ridiculed, mocked and persecuted the prophets, and as a result were engulfed by God's judgment while the prophets and the faithful were saved[37].

At the same time biblical stories were increasingly interpreted through the contextual prism of Arab culture, [s38]as Muhammad drew similarities between the biblical and the Arab prophets. This characterization of prophetic history provided the framework in which Muhammad was able to interpret his own experience of being God's contemporary messenger to the Arabs in continuity with both Arab and biblical prophets of the past. He set his preaching and his suffering at the recalcitrance of the Meccan people against the measure of the life and work of previous messengers. Mecca was also compared to the previous communities who had rejected the divine message and turned their backs against God's prophets. Mutatis mutandis, the stories of the previous messengers of God were adapted more and more to the contours of Muhammad's situation, and earlier generations of unbelievers provided a metaphor for the pagan Meccans and their impending fate.

Clearly, these stories reflect Muhammad's context and are shaped by it. Muhammad did not consider his message to be something new or special, since its veracity depended on it being essentially the same as that of the previous prophets. All of the prophets -Muhammad included- received their revelation directly from the one and only God who calls all human communities to worship Him alone. By the same argument, Muhammad understood his message to be a confirmation of the previous prophets[39]. The claim of uniqueness had no place in this scheme. On the other hand, Muhammad was contextually conscious of his particularity: that he was sent to a community or people who had not been graced in earlier history by a messenger from God[40], and to whom no scripture had previously been granted[41].

B.
The Qur'an - a holy liturgy in Arabic

In the above mentioned verse, God addresses Muhammad regarding the Meccans in the following terms,

"And We have not granted them any scripts (previously), in which they could have searched, nor have We sent messengers to them before you to warn them." [42]

The first sentence of this verse is evidence that Muhammad did not know of the existence of any scripture in Arabic, either an original Arabic scripture or an Arabic translation of the Bible. Yet he was obviously aware of the important status that scripture enjoyed in both Jewish and Christian traditions of worship. He would have been familiar with the sight of Arabian Jews reciting the Torah in Hebrew and was aware that the various Christian peoples of Syria, Egypt and Arabia recited the Bible in their own languages.

The recitation of scripture was an indispensable element in the worship of God in both Jewish and Christian religious traditions in the Middle East. Indeed it gave rise to and became the essential component of liturgy. Prior to Muhammad, an Arabic liturgy did not exist. The Arab peoples had nothing to compare with the liturgical wealth of their Jewish and Christian neighbors. This was the source of much concern for Muhammad as he sought to bring his people to worship God in the true way. It was to remedy this impoverishment that he emphasized the priority of an "Arabic Qur'an."

As mentioned, the word qur'an denotes something which is recited, words that are spoken aloud, and a message that is chanted. In its Semitic context, this concept qur'an appears to derive from an Aramaic precedent, where the term qeryana denoted any biblical text sung as part of the liturgy of the Syrian Church[43]. A parallel concept is found in Jewish rabbinical literature in what Hebrew -calls miqra. This is used in the Talmud to refer to the whole Jewish Bible, serving "to underline both the vocal manner of study and the central role the public reading of the scriptures played in the liturgy of the Jews"[44]. These terminological explanations suggest a concept of the way the Bible functions in worship that differs greatly from contemporary(especially Protestant) practice in the West. Recent research, however, has shown that the Western concept of scripture as something silently read and privately studied is a relatively recent phenomenon.

There is substantial evidence "that it is in only relatively recent history and specifically in the modern West that the book has become a silent object, the written work a silent sign, and the reader a silent spectator."[45]

The biblical practice with which Muhammad would have been familiar in indigenous Jewish and Christian liturgies was a "community book" something which was chanted in worship. In this sense, were Muhammad alive today, he would arguably be more at home in a Middle Easterner Jewish or Christian liturgy than would the average Western Jew or Christian. It is reasonable, therefore, to conjecture that as Muhammad sought to persuade his people to worship God, it would have been with a liturgical concept of scripture

Contextualizing the Scripture 61

with which he attempted to remedy what was lacking in their cultural heritage. It might almost be said that in contrast to wishing to create a new religion with its own scripture, he intended to establish a local Arabic "liturgy" (qeryana, miqra, qur'an) comparable to that which the Jewish and Christian recipients of previous scriptures enjoyed.

An analysis of the form and composition of the qur'anic suras confirms this perspective. As Angelica Neuwirth has noted in her book, *Studien zur Komposition der Mekkanischen Suren*, the Qur'an was originally constructed as a liturgical speech and a recited text. She shows that Muhammad was aware that various religious groups had already evolved this practice of scripture. That which was common to the liturgical practices of these groups were the elements of introit, prayers and songs in between prayers, all of which were based on the words of scripture. Neuwirth argues that the form in which the qur'anic suras are composed is best understood within the comparative history of liturgy in the Middle East, where historic custom set scripture inseparably in the context of liturgical worship[46].

Neuwirth applied her thesis in a detailed study on the opening chapter of the Qur'an, Surat al-Fatiha. Rather than reading it as the introduction to a book, she interprets it as the introit to "prayer liturgy." Prayer(salah) was the essential element of the developing Islamic cult, of worship during the Meccan period, and quickly became the distinguishing feature of the group of converts who surrounded the Prophet. The content of their prayers comprised verses of the Qur'an which were recited from memory in the as-yet entirely oral tradition of retaining holy words[47]. The Fatiha was the primary form of such prayer, and has continued to be so in Muslim practice throughout history. The link between prayer and recitation led Neuwirth to conclude that the organizational format of the Quran should be understood "in the context of the familiar forms used for the opening ceremony of the communal services at Prophet Muhammad's time"[48].

Related to this important insight into the liturgical nature of the Qur'an is the fact that it was/is an Arabic liturgy(qur'an 'arabi) as the Qur'an several times emphasizes by way of self-definition[49]. This raises the issue of language as an essential ingredient of contextualization. As has already been shown, Muhammad was convinced during the Meccan period of his preaching that his message was identified in content with earlier prophets and particularly to the Jews and Christians who are known collectively in the Qur'an as the ahl al-kitab, "the People of the Book." The message he was preaching differed from these biblical scriptures in one respect only, namely the language in which it was revealed and communicated. It was an Arabic Qur'an, accepted and internalized by Arab converts, who then reflected on its meaning in prayerful liturgy in the Arabic language. The fact that it was in Arabic, the language of the people, was inseparably connected in Muhammad's mind with its quality as revealed truth.

To understand this connection it is helpful to examine closely a verse in Surat Fussilat[50] which reads:

> "Should we have had it, a Qur'an(in a language) other than Arabic, they would have said: 'why its verses are not explained(separately) - a non-Arabic Qur'an and an Arabic(messenger)!' Say: For all who believe, it is guidance and a healing. For those who do not believe it causes deafness in the ears, and it deprives them of their sight. They are people who are being called from afar." [51]

At one level this verse speaks unambiguously to the cultural imperative that scripture be in the language of the people in order that it be understood. A Qur'an in the indigenous Arabic language was a condition of its being understood by the Arab people to whom it was revealed, and thus an aid for their belief[52]. Beyond the level of comprehension, however, the concept of the Qur'an as an Arabic, liturgy allows for a more profound dimension of meaning. A liturgy enacted in a foreign language is deprived of the power to affect, impress and transform the worshipper. The word of God, as it were, remains in the dark - silent, inconceivable.

In Christian experience, a local liturgy corresponds with the Christian concept of Incarnation. As Jesus' disciples believed that in Jesus they had seen into the mystery of God - into God's manner of revealing divinity to them, of God's being with them in Jesus' person, actions and words - so later generations of Christians have continued to encounter God-in-Christ in the divine liturgy. Does this ancient Christian understanding of the spiritual significance of liturgy afford an insight into the meaning of the Qur'an? In the concluding sentence of the above-quoted verse, the unbelievers(whose hearing and sight have been made useless) are said to be a people who are being called from a distant place. By contrast, those who believe, and for whom, therefore, the Qur'an provides guidance and healing, must be understood as experiencing God's Word as an immediate, intimate reality – actually present in words of the Arabic Qur'an. This surely implies Muhammad and following his precedence, all devout Muslims experiencing God calling them in and through the Qur'an, near and clear, not "from afar" where, for the unbeliever, God remains remote.

The Qur'an thus becomes for Muslims the point of divine-human encounter, just as divine liturgy has traditionally been the same for Middle Eastern Christianity. In the Middle Eastern Churches revelation has never been related primarily to text, but rather to the liturgy which is characterized as "holy". God makes His presence known in liturgy as the presence of Jesus Christ is known in the celebrated sacrament. In this respect Cantwell Smith is correct in drawing a comparison between the Muslim recital of the Qur'an and the Christian celebration of the Eucharist[53].

This means of understanding the liturgical quality of the Arabic Qur'an also addresses another issue upon which Islamic orthodoxy insists: that the Qur'an is not to be translated. Translation is of course technically possible albeit fraught with philological perils. The Qur'an has been effectively translated into many languages for purposes of human understanding though not for authoritative reference in matters of faith and ethics. Yet by the criterion of a liturgical understanding of the holy quality of the Qur'an, a purely cognitive approach to the text as implied in the question of translation is clearly inadequate. Translation cannot transmit the proximity of God which is experienced in the liturgical recitation of the Qur'an in Arabic. A translated text does not touch the soul; it cannot inspire people to meditate, pray and weep - or as the Qur'an puts it:

"When the verses of [God] Most Gracious are recited to them, they fall down prostrate in adoration and in tears." [54]

Though intellectual meaning may be conveyed through translation, the spiritual quality of the text is dulled; it remains distant and becomes, as it is for unbelievers, something which merely "calls from afar."

Revealed scripture by this liturgical reckoning cannot be translated because it would lose its revelatory quality. That which applies to the translation of the Arabic Qur'an into another language is the same logic which would have constrained Muhammad from translating the Bible from its original languages into Arabic. Muhammad claimed recognition as a prophet, not as a Bible translator[55]. Eager as he may have been to learn as much as possible of the Jewish and Christian scriptures, and convinced that the message he was preaching was essentially the same as theirs, his specific vocation was to render divine revelation to the Arabs in their own tongue. The Arabic Qur'an could not be the scriptural liturgy for Arabs that Muhammad intended if it were merely a translation of Hebrew, Aramaic and Greek texts.

All revelation needs to be culturally specific, both in language and content. In this sense the Arabs needed "a new revelation" and the Qur'an calls to be recognized as such. This is the logic of a decentralized concept of revelation. Revelation, in the early qur'anic understanding is re-iterated in culturally-specific forms linguistically diverse but united in the message it conveys. The preaching of God's word is not controlled by a single authoritative center which sends missionaries out to disseminate and translate the message; rather, it is communicated by many local prophets who proclaim the message to their people. A processed "indigenization" is redundant because the messengers and the message are already indigenous. As the Qur'an puts it,

"And We have sent you no messenger (to any nation), except (with a message) in the languages of its people, so as he can offer them clarity."[56]

It is the linguistic clarity of qur'anic scripture, and its liturgical impact through which God's presence is known and celebrated, that infuses the Qur'an with the quality of "inimitability" or "uniqueness" – i'jaz in Arabic, which Muslim religious scholars have applied to both its form and content.

The Qur'an in Medina

The suras belonging to the Meccan periods of Muhammad's preaching were not then understood as constituting a new scripture, independent of the scriptures of the Jews and Christians. It has been argued that they should be understood, instead, as a form of liturgical contextualization of God's word, parallel to the Jewish and Christian liturgies with which Muhammad would have been familiar. Muhammad vehemently rejected the taunt of pagan Meccans who claimed that they would not believe anything he had to say until and unless he brought them a book that they could read[57]. The idea of a new scripture was tantamount to disbelief. After the Hijra from Mecca to Medina in 622 AD, Muhammad was faced with a new context which required new responses. The concept of a prophet for his own qawm(people, or tribe) no longer pertained to the confined, localized sense it originally had in Mecca. His own people tribe of Quraish had repudiated him, whereas another people, the tribe of Medina, welcomed him and many became his devout followers. The message, consequently, had to be broadened and expanded beyond Mecca. The situation in Medina differed also in that its population included several resident Jewish tribes. This gave Muhammad his first sustained contact with Jews with whom, as "the People of the Book"(ahl al-kitab) he had identified himself spiritually while in Mecca. As he encountered them in Medina, however, he was quickly disappointed on two counts. They rejected his credentials as a prophet with the same message as theirs, and with Abraham and Moses in particular; and they argued among themselves which suggested to Muhammad that they were in disagreement about the revelation which they had received from their prophets - the very prophet whose missions Muhammad invoked in authentication of his own. The rejection of Muhammad's claim to be a prophet was especially painful since it came not from pagans but from those whom he regarded as fellow believers. This forced him to rethink his position and develop a new orientation in two major areas. First, he needed to re-define his understanding of the relationship between his message and that of the People of the Book who rejected it. Second, he had to explain the divisions among the People of the Book themselves. These two existential issues caste in a new light what had been a key premise of his teaching during the Meccan period: namely, that the message of the various prophets is universally identical. Were this the case, Muhammad must now have asked himself, surely the faith of the Jewish tribes would have led them to recognize his status as a prophet of God? Unity among the followers of a monotheistic tradition of faith should have also resulted. In that this was evidently not the case on either count, the Meccan teachings had to undergo modification and expansion.

With this context in mind, it is possible to examine the development of Muhammad's teaching in relation to his understanding of scripture and the concept of "a chosen people." The scenario in which the evolution took place was evidently one of dispute with the Medinan Jew though by extension it applied to Christians as well. In contrast to the harmonious spirit of the Meccan suras, the Medinan passages of relevance to this discussion are of a more disputatious nature. It is noteworthy that the line of Muhammad's argument displays interesting parallels with earlier religious controversies, evident in the texts of the New Testament between emergent Christianity and Judaism.

A.
The Qur'an - a "furqan" for former scriptures

According to the evidence of Islamic historical texts, it seems likely that Muhammad had direct discussions with Jewish rabbis[58]. In these debates the rabbis would have produced many arguments to dismiss Muhammad's claim that the Qur'an was identical to the Torah. Muhammad, for his part, would have argued the obverse proposition, that it was the Torah which was out of harmony with the Qur'an.

This involved several explanations. A small but significant qualification was introduced into the qur'anic description of "the People of the Book" from the original "those, who were granted scriptures," to those who were granted part [nasib] of the scriptures,"[59] This in effect reduced the Torah, in qur'anic estimation, to the status of a partial and, therefore, imperfect scripture by comparison with the Qur'an which contained the full account of God's word.

It was in this Medinan context that Muhammad first employed the terms tawrat and injil[60] to distinguish two discrete scriptures - the Torah and the Gospel - neither of which was deemed to be complete inspiration of the Word of God. A second line of argument focused on the human stewardship of scripture. The Jews in particular were reproached for allegedly having distorted their scripture[61]. The Qur'an, by contrast, professed to be a perfect book, qualified therefore to function as the criterion of divine truth against which the shortcomings of earlier scriptures could be exposed[62]. The term furqan denotes this discriminatory function, establishing the authoritative canon by which the true word of God is established. The Qur'an thus became an independent scripture, differentiated from both the tawrat of the Jews and the injil of the Christians. No longer did it serve only as an Arabic liturgy, but came to be construed as a holy book(kitab), comprising revelations which henceforth were to be recorded and compiled - though the textual result was fully established only after Muhammad's death.

B.
The Qur'an - a revelation for the "pagan"

Muhammad interpreted his rejection by the Jews as evidence not only of their mis-understanding of scripture but also as the error of their own self-understanding of being a "chosen people"[63]. It is with respect to the latter perspective that the Jews denounced Muhammad and characterized the Muslim community in Medina as "pagan"[64]. The term ummiyyun is the Arabic equivalent of the Hebrew ummot, meaning "pagan peoples." Although for the Jews it carried pejorative implications, Mohammad accepted the term and infused it with a positive meaning. Using the singular form of the word he referred to himself as al-nabi al-ummi. This clearly did not mean that he regarded himself as in any way a "pagan" prophet, but rather a prophet called by God from outside the ranks of those who regarded themselves as God's specially chosen: a prophet for those who, by the standards of the Medinan Jews at least, were marginalized from God's workings in history[65]. For the reader of the New Testament, this recalls the Apostle Paul's styling himself, when faced by the rejection of his fellow Jews, as the "pagan" prophet sent to the Gentiles. In a comparable manner, Muhammad turned consciously away from the Jews and identified himself and his mission specifically in relation to the Arab ummiyyun.

If his rejection by the Jews was the historical contingency which prompted this change, Muhammad's decision was entirely consistent with his understanding of a decentralized Heilsgeschichte. The Qur'an therefore claims that Muhammad was predicted to fulfill the role of al-nabi al-'umi in both the tawrat and the injil[66] - in the former by Abraham who is said to have petitioned God to send the Meccans an indigenous prophet[67], and in the latter by Jesus who is said to have predicted the advent of a prophet named Ahmad[68] whom Muslim scholars identify as Muhammad. Muslim scholars have seen in this qur'anic reference an insinuation of the Paraclete references in the Gospel of John[69].

A further criticism of the Jews' exclusivist understanding of Heilsgeschichte is found in the importance the Qur'an attaches to the prophet Ishmael(Isma'il) in the Medinan period of Muhammad's ministry. Already mentioned in the Meccan verses, his specific role as a prophet was not elaborated; he is simply included among other prophets[70] without any specific link to Abraham being established. This latter connection is only elaborated in the Medinan passages of the Qur'an, most importantly in the story of Abraham's(re) building of the ka'ba in Mecca[71]. The reason for this may again be found in the context of Muhammad's controversy with the Medinan Jews. It is certainly not difficult to imagine the latter, considering themselves to be the "chosen people" proudly parading their genealogical lineage as the descendants of Abraham and Isaac before Muhammad and disparaging the Arabs for being merely the descendants of Ishmael. This, after all, is consistent with the view of the Hebrew scriptures which has God's Heilsgeschichte run selectively from Abraham through Isaac to Jacob, and in effect writes Ishmael out of the story[72]. Muhammad's genius is that he took up the cause of the excluded and marginalized[73]. In Medina he thus focused much more specifically on the mission of the prophet Ishmael who now assumed a status fully equal to that of Isaac[74]. Each of these references includes an important phrase: "We make no distinction between one and another among them." The Qur'an's decentralized Heilsgeschichte therefore places all the prophets - Isaac and Ishmael included -in equal rank in the sight of God. Ishmael was rescued from the shadows of Jewish Heilsgeschichte, and with him the Arabs were given equal status with the Jews.

It is important to note that the qur'anic phrase, "We make no distinction between one and other among them [i.e. the prophets]," applies not only to Isaac and Ishmael. In the two occurrences of the phrase cited in the previous paragraph, specific mention is made also of Moses and Jesus. This clearly raises a question against the Christian understanding of Jesus, though this is not the issue I propose to pursue here.[75] Within the present discussion, the attribution of equal status for Moses and Jesus serves a different purpose. It places each prophet and their followers - Jews and Christians respectively - in an equal relationship with Abraham.

Abraham, in the Meccan suras, was the paradigm of the hanif, an Arabic word, probably of Syriac derivation whose original meaning (either "pagan" or "true believer") is disputed by scholars[76]. In its qur'anic usage, it conveys the sense of "one who is God-fearing" and denotes anyone, regardless of religious creed, who professes belief in the monotheistic God and lives in ethical obedience to Him. The word is used paradigmatically of Abraham, against the background of the story of his break with the polytheistic traditions of his father's religion[77]. In the Medinan elaboration of the quality of Abraham's faith, hanif becomes the defining characteristic of the religious community (milla) which comes to be identified with Abraham - the milla ibrahim.

In the context of Muhammad's dispute with the Jews (and by extension the Christians), this characterization of Abraham's religion provided a basis on which to debate the question of legitimate descent. The dynamics of the argument are clear in the Qur'an passage which reads,

> *"They [the People of the Book say: You have to be Jew or Christian if you are to be on the path [of salvation]. Say: No! [For us there is only] the religion of Abraham, a hanif, who was not one of the idolaters."* [78]

This argument against salvific privilege on the basis of religion was designed to counter theological opposition by the People of the Book to Muhammad's message. For those familiar with the New Testament, this again echoes an argument of the Apostle Paul in relation to his dispute with Jewish rabbis who claimed that the legacy of Abraham was confined exclusively to Jews who had been circumcised into God's covenant with Abraham.

On the basis of his exegesis of Genesis 15 to 17, Paul argued that Abraham's faith was deemed righteous before he was circumcised; hence faith, not circumcision, is the true mark of Abrahamic righteousness. Muhammad was making a similar point, this time against both Jews and Christians:

> *"You People of the Book: why are you quarrelling over Abraham when the Torah and the Gospel were only sent after his time? Have you no understanding? ... Abraham was neither Jew nor Christian. Rather, he was hanif who submitted to God and was not an idolater."* [79]

A further ramification of this argument began to change the original qur'anic view of a decentralized Heilsgeschichte. The concept of "Islam" in the Medinan portions of the Qur'an is gradually transformed from the attitude toward God shown by the God-fearing hanif, of whom Abraham was the exemplar par excellence, to become the crystallization of the religion and religious community(mill) which Abraham led. Muhammad identified himself with this community in unambiguous terms:

> *"Say: My Lord has guided me to a straight path, an established religion, the religion of Abraham, a hanif who was not an idolater ... Truly, my prayer and my sacrifice, my life and my death are all for God, the Lord of the Worlds. No partner has He. Of this I am commanded, and I am the first of those who submit [i.e. muslims."* [80]

C.
The Qur'an - a contextual legislation for a new religion

The process of differentiation between Islam and the earlier religions of Judaism and Christianity did not take place solely at the level of theological debate. The debate itself was set in the context of the expansion of the Muslim community in Medina as the Medinan Arab tribes converted enmasse to Muhammad's teaching. Islam was rapidly becoming a definition: community, with requirements of community identity and structure. Externally it was locked in conflict with the Meccan oligarchy of Quraish whose tribal leaders

Contextualizing the Scripture 73

engaged in an economic war with Medina over control of the Arabian track routes. As Muhammad prevailed in this contest, more and more of the Arabian tribes looked to Medina as the centre of a new Arabian empire, whose socio-political power was rooted in Muhammad's religious teaching.

Another aspect of Islam's disengagement from Judaism is evident in the ritual sphere of religious self-definition. It is in Medina, therefore, that Islam emerges with a distinctive cult, centered upon symbols which were a deep part of local Arab culture.

The key feature of the emerging Islamic cult was the ka'ba, an ancient cube-shaped sanctuary in Mecca, the origins of which doubtlessly belong to indigenous traditions of Arabian tribal religion. Already mentioned in the earliest Meccan portions of the Qur'an as the sanctuary specifically associated with the Quraish[81], the ka'ba takes on much greater significance once Muhammad is in Medina where its origins are linked to the missions of Abraham and Ishmael[82]. The ka'ba was covered as it were, with the tapestry of Abraham's story to which, for reasons already discussed, Ishmael's was linked. As Abraham's religion was the paradigmatic form of monotheism, so the ka'ba became the original shrine of monotheistic worship. The Qur'an is not clear as to when or by whom it was built. Did Abraham himself, assisted by Ishmael[83], build it or did they simply restore and cleanse an already existent sanctuary[84], constructed by someone else, which had fallen into idolatrous misuse by their day? The lack of a historical answer to this question need not concern us, however, since it is the cultic significance of the ka'ba with which the Qur'an is concerned in the critical passage mentioned earlier and now quoted in full.

It takes the form of a prayer which Abraham and Ishmael are said to have prayed by the side of the ka'ba at a place referred to since then as "Abraham's place of prayer"(musalla Ibrahim) or alternatively,(maqam Ibrahim), "the place where Abraham stood":

> *"Lord, accept [this] from us [both]. You are the One who hears and knows all. Make us submissive to You (muslimin) and let our descend¬ants become a community submissive to You(umma muslima). And show us our rites. And turn to us in mercy, for You are the merciful and compassionate."* [85]

Of the rites here in question the most important is that of pilgrimage (hajj). This was originally an ancient Arab cultic festival performed at the ka'ba. Now, in a process of symbolic transference, it was given new meaning in association with Abraham and Ishmael who in turn are robed in purified Arab cultic garb. It was no coincidence that Muhammad physically purified the ka'ba of all idolatrous associations as his first act after Mecca's capitulation to Islam in 630 AD.

The continuation of Abraham's prayer at the kab'a says:

> *"Lord, send among them [i.e. the descendants of Abraham and Ishmael] a messenger from their own ranks, who will recite Your signs [revealed verses] to them, who will instruct them in the scripture and wisdom, and purify them [from the pollution of paganism]. You are the Almighty and the All-wise."* [86]

This prayer draws us to "the heart of the matter" in understanding how Muhammad must have perceived himself and the religious community which he created. He was the nabi al-ummi - the prophet for the Arabs who had been excluded from the biblical Heilsgeschichte. Like Ishmael, whom the Jews had marginalized from God's purposes in history, his prophethood was impugned and his preaching criticized. He responded with a radical act of local contextualization, consistent with the decentralized Heilsgeschiche which he had developed from his earliest preaching in Mecca. Abraham was not the patriarch of a single people, but "the leader of humankind[87] who, by association with his son Ishmael could bear a distinctly Arab identity while at the same time being the father of Isaac, the progenitor of the Jews. The symbolism of this identity focused cultically on the ka'ba and the rites of prayer(salah) and pilgrimage (hajj). Muhammad saw himself as the embodiment of this contextualization of Abrahamic history and his followers as its communal realization.

Conclusion

By re-reading the Qur'an in a text-critical and contextual way, the different developments in qur'anic self-understanding become clear. In the Meccan period one can see the Qur'an as a warning to the people of Mecca, Muhammad as a prophet to the Arabs, and the Qur'an as an Arab Judeo-Christian liturgy. A positive attitude towards the Jewish and Christian scriptures in particular can be seen during this period. In the Madinan period, the Qur'an is increasingly distinguished from previous scriptures. It begins to function as a criterion by which the formed are judged. It is a revelation to the "pagans" - those outside the Judeo Christian Heilsgeschichte, and a cultic law for the newly established Muslim community. It is interesting in this regard to see how the Qur'an deals with the biblical heritage, including the Arabization of the scripture, the enculturation of Biblical stories and the contextualization of Jewish- Christian theology and methodology. This process was shaped by the interaction of three different elements, namely: Arab culture, the Judeo-Christian heritage, and the experience of the Prophet himself. In all stages of this process one can see an obvious tendency to Arabize and to contextualize the

Judeo-Christian heritage. In this regard, the Prophet Mohammed can be viewed as a master of contextual theology and the Qur'an as the scripture for Arab tribes.

4.

The Evangelical Lutheran Church in Jordan and the Holy Land Past[1] and Present

I.
Introduction

The Evangelical Lutheran Church in Jordan and the Holy Land (ELCJHL) is the result of the attempt to reform the Middle Eastern Churches. As Luther's attempt to reform the Roman Catholic Church in Europe resulted in the establishment of a new church, here too the outcome of the Protestant Missions in Palestine was not the reformation of these Churches but the formation of a new one.

The Lutheran Reformation emerged from a European Roman Catholic context, and remained contained for a long period within the boundaries of Western Europe. However, the existence of the Eastern Churches was well-known to the reformers. Their existence supported and strengthened Martin Luther's conviction that the Roman Catholic Church was not the sole representative of the Christian faith as the Middle Eastern Churches were at least as old.

Contact between the newly established German Lutheran Church and the Eastern Churches, particularly the Greek Orthodox

Church, began in 1559 when the Patriarch of Constantinople, Joasaph II, seeking further information about the Reformation, sent his deacon Demetrios Mysos, to Wittenberg. In Wittenberg Demetrios met with Phillip Melanchthon, a close associate of Martin Luther who gave him a Greek translation of his *Confessio Augustana*, the summary of Lutheran theology. No response, however, was forthcoming from Constantinople.[2]

A second contact to the Patriarch of Constantinople, Jeremias II, was initiated approximately fourteen years later by two theologians from Tubingen, Martin Crusius and Jacob Andrea, resulting in a weighty dialogue. That dialogue was discontinued in 1581 when the Patriarch wrote that discussions concerning dogmas are futile.[3]

Further contacts did not take place again until the beginning of the 19th century after Napoleon's invasion in 1799. These meetings emerged from the new context of European presence in the Middle East which simultaneously was marked by a strong religious awakening resulting in worldwide mission work. Although the mission work was directed towards the conversion of "heathens" some mission societies soon decided to begin work in the Middle East, a region where only followers of the three monotheistic religions were to be found.

II.
The First Protestant Missionaries in Palestine

In 1808 the London Missionary Society sent a missionary to Malta in order "to reawaken the pure religion in the Greek Orthodox Church."[4] In the same year the London Jews Society was established to relieve "the temporal distress of the Jews and the promotion of their welfare."[5] Several years later the American Board of Commissioners for Foreign Missions decided to begin mission work in Palestine and in 1819 sent their first two missionaries.[6] One aim of these missionaries was the revival of the Oriental Churches. Until the end of the 1820s "little or nothing has been attempted in Jerusalem; the visits of all the missionaries have been for short periods,"[7] as foreigners were forbidden by the Ottoman Empire to own land or even to reside in Jerusalem. In 1824 an Ottoman firman prohibited the import and circulation of Bibles and Psalms printed in Europe because they "instigated unrest and unnecessary disputes."[8]

The Work of Missionary Nicolayson during the Era of Muhammad Ali

The year 1831 is of great importance to the history of Protestant missions in Palestine. In that year Ibrahim Pasha, the son of Muhammad Ali, invaded Palestine which began a new era of secularism and nationalism in the history of Palestine. Mission work benefited from these dramatic changes. In 1832 Ibrahim declared that "Muslims and Christians are all our subjects. The question of religion has no connection with political considerations. (In religious matters) every individual must be left alone. The believer to practice his Islam and the Christian his Christianity. But no one to have authority over the other. "[9] Under these circumstances mission work was tolerated. "The Christian missionary enjoys perfect liberty to carry on his operation under the Egyptian Government, more so indeed than under the British government at Malta or India".[10]

By late 1833 Nicholayson, a missionary sent by the London Jews Society was able, for the first time, to rent a house in Jerusalem. He performed services both in Hebrew and in Arabic. In 1839 he wrote: "Some native Christians, both of the Latin and Greek Church, being regular attendants at the Arabic service are anxious to fully join our Church... I have hitherto succeeded in putting them off, and shall endeavor to do so till we get perfectly organized and have a location of our own."[11] In 1838, the same year of the establishment of an English Consulate in Jerusalem, Nicholayson purchased two plots of Episcopal authority[12] and on February 10, 1840, he laid the cornerstone for a church; interestingly enough not in the Jewish Quarter but in the Armenian Quarter.

Shortly thereafter the rule of Ibrahim Pasha came to an end, when the European powers assisted the Ottoman Empire in regaining control of Palestine. Due to European assistance, the Ottoman rulers were receptive to reforms in the fields of politics, society, and religion.[13] The presence of Europeans, including their missionaries, was permitted.

III
The Bishopic of the United Church of England and Ireland in Jerusalem[14]

There were various perspectives on the European presence in Palestine after the reestablishment of Ottoman rule. One which was particularly important for the formation of the Evangelical Lutheran Church was the new plan put forth by the King of Prussia, Friedrich Wilhelm IV. The King was extremely well-informed about the work of missionary Nicoholayson, about the building of Christ Church, and about the desire of some Palestinian Christians to join

Protestantism. At the same time he was aware of the difficulty facing these Christians, as Protestantism was not officially recognized in the Ottoman millet system.[15] This system was not individually oriented but rather community oriented. "It was based on the concept that law was personal rather than territorial and that religion rather than either domicile or political allegiance determined the law under which an individual lived."[16] As long as Protestantism was an unrecognized community, conversion into the community was almost impossible. The King's goal was "to obtain for Protestants already settled in Turkey, whether foreigners or Ottoman subjects, 'securities and protection similar to those which Christians of other denominations enjoy'."[17] He desired securing the recognition of Protestantism in the Ottoman Empire as millet, and was convinced that only through a united Protestant Church would this recognition be possible.[18] At the same time he attempted to establish a German Protestant Bishopric in Bethlehem[19] and to further these goals he sent his delegate, Bunsen, to London to ask the Anglican Church to establish a Bishopric in Jerusalem in which the United (Lutheran Reformed) Prussian Church would participate. An agreement was reached on July 19, 1841, which was signed on December 7, 1841. It was agreed to send a Bishop to Jerusalem who would be nominated alternatively by the crowns of England and Prussia. Two days later a "Statement of Proceeding" from this agreement was published, outlining the duties of the Bishop:

> *"His chief missionary care will be directed to the conversion of the Jews, to their protection, and to their useful employment. He will establish and maintain, as far as in him lies, relations of Christian charity with other churches represented at Jerusalem, and in particular with the Orthodox Greek Church; taking special care to convince them, that the Church of England does not wish to disturb, or divide, or interfere with them; but that she is ready, in*

the spirit of Christian love, to render them such offices of friendship as they may be willing to receive."[20]

Comparing the King of Prussia's instructions to Bunsen and the "Statement of Proceeding" there is a slight change regarding converting Jews.

For fulfilling the mission as laid out in the "Statement of Proceedings" a converted Jew was considered to be the most capable candidate. Therefore, Professor Dr. Michael Salomon Alexander[21] was chosen as the first Anglican bishop sent to Jerusalem in January 21, 1842. Bishop Alexandar earnestly endeavored to meet the obligations of the "Statement of Proceedings." He concentrated on converting Jews, and was eager to maintain good relations with the Oriental Churches. When therefore, some Greek Orthodox Christians from Hasbay, Lebanon in 1844 asked to join the Anglican Church, he refused them. This refusal was not understood by the King of Prussia who asked his delegate to negotiate this matter with the Head of the Anglican Church.[22] For several reasons this negotiation never took place, and on November 26, 1845 Bishop Alexander died. The Prussian King then nominated Samuel Gobat to succeed him.

IV.
Samuel Gobat and the Establishment of the First Arab Protestant Congregations[23]

Without the work of Bishop Gobat there would today be no Arab Protestant congregations in Palestine. For it was he who shifted the emphasis from converting Jews to the reformation of the

Oriental Churches. In retrospect, it was as if Bishop Gobat was predestined for such work among these churches. Even before being appointed Bishop of Jerusalem, he had concentrated his efforts in this area. As a missionary of the English Church Missionary Society, he started his work revising Arabic missionary brochures, because he had mastered Arabic. In 1827 he witnessed the establishment of the first Arabic, Protestant congregation in Beirut; from 1829 until 1838 he worked as a missionary in Abyssinia where he had already developed the concept of reforming the Oriental Churches.[24] It is interesting to ponder if the King of Prussia appointed Gobat Bishop precisely because of his convictions and missionary work. Shortly after entering Jerusalem on December 30, 1846, Bishop Gobat started circulating Bibles among members of the Eastern Churches. This circulation introduced individual reading as well as Bible study; new methods in the Eastern Churches as the Bible was mainly the book of the Liturgy. Since most people were illiterate at that time, he first opened schools. These schools were called "Bible Schools," as the Bible was the main teaching tool.[25]

During his time as Bishop in Jerusalem, Bishop Gobat was able to establish twenty-five Protestant schools in Palestine, two of which are Lutheran schools today.[26] Attacked by High Church oriented groups in England for his concept of reformation of the Eastern Churches, Bishop Gobat threatened to resign if the Archbishop of Canterbury would not clarify the policy of how the Bishop in Jerusalem was to handle the members of the Eastern Churches wishing to join the Anglican Church. On October 16, 1850, the Archbishop of Canterbury and the Prussian delegate, Bunsen, undersigned just such an official policy. This policy distinguished between proselytism and Christian witness: "The difference is great between an aggressive system of Polemical efforts to detach the members of a communion from it, and a calm exposition of Scriptural truth and quiet exhibition of Scriptural discipline. Duty requires the latter; and where it has pleased God to give his blessing to it, and the mind has become emancipated from the fetters of a corrupt faith, there we have no right to turn our backs upon the liberated captive, and bid him return to his slavery, or seek aid elsewhere. It is desirable nevertheless wherever a sufficient number of individuals may have left the Greek Church to form a separate distinct reformed congregation of the Greek Church, not as a congregation of the Church of England, and to assist them in the compilation and use of such a Liturgy as best suit their circumstances, and to left it be understood that if Ministers in English Orders minister among them it is to prevent their entire destitution, but that if any of their own Priests should become of like mind with themselves, their ministrations would be made available."[27] In the same year a firman was granted by the Turkish Sultan "granting protection to Protestants, being Turkish subjects."[28] As a result of these two documents Bishop Gobat was able to follow his vision of establishing a "Protestant National Church" in Palestine.[29] By the time of his death in 1879 Bishop Gobat had established twelve Protestant congregations in the Holy Land.[30]

In addition to building schools and establishing congregations, Bishop Gobat also requested that various German mission societies come to Palestine and begin work. In order to coordinate work between the German and the English missionary societies, Bishop Gobat established a gentleman's agreement between the two. In this agreement northern Palestine was declared the mission field for English missionaries while southern Palestine was for the Germans.[31] Due to this division Lutheran congregations are today found mainly south of Jerusalem, while Anglican congregations lie in the north. The work of three German societies, which began under Bishop Gobat, was crucial to the establishment of the Lutheran Church.

V.
The Work of the German Mission Societies in Palestine

A.
The Work of the Kaiserwerth Deaconesses

In 1850 an epidemic swept across Jerusalem. In response, Bishop Gobat asked Theodor Fliedner, the director of the Kaiserwerth Deaconesses' House, to send deaconesses to begin work in Jerusalem. On May 4, 1851, two deaconesses dedicated the first Protestant hospital. On the same day two other deaconesses opened a girl's school which was called Talitha Kumi. By choosing this name the concept of deaconesses was emphasized; the awakening of the Arab woman.[32]

B.
The Work of Johann Ludwig Schneller and the Establishment of the Syrian Orphanage

Schneller came to Palestine in 1854 sent by the Basel Mission to direct the Basel Brother House in Jerusalem. Several years later, however, Schneller left his directorship and began work on his own vision. Witnessing the massacre of Christians in Syria in 1860, he felt the need to care for children orphaned in the massacre; his goal was to establish an institution where orphans would be able to develop into productive members of society as well as be active members of the church. For the realization of this goal he emphasized Christian education and vocational training. "Ora et labora" was his motto.[33]

C.
The Work of the Jerusalem Society

In 1860 Bishop Gobat asked the Jerusalem Society, a foundation established in Berlin in 1852, to take care of the Arab Protestant congregations in southern Palestine[34], while the English Church Missionary Society concerned itself with those in northern Palestine. The Jerusalem Society took over the congregations and schools of Bethlehem in 1860, and established new institutions in Beit Jala in 1879[35], in Hebron in 1884[36], in Beit Sahour in 1900[37], and in Jerusalem in 1903[38].

VI.
The Breakdown of the Joint Bishopric

In 1879 Bishop Gobat died and was succeeded by Jospeh Barclay, a former London Jews Society missionary. Barclay was appointed by Queen Victoria and sought to redirect the work of the Jerusalem Bishopric from the reformation of Eastern Christians to the conversion of Jews and extended that mission among Muslims.[39]

However, he only had two years at his post before his death in October 1881. The Germans did not feel the need to continue the joint Bishopric. After the creation of Germany by Bismarck in 1871, the Germans, with considerable power in Europe, did not wish to be as subordinates to England especially as German mission work in Palestine was flourishing and even surpassing the English. Thus on November 3, 1886, the joint Bishopric ended. The Jerusalem Bishopric continued for the English missions, while the Germans missions had no umbrella of authority under which to work.[40] The Kaiser's previous idea of creating an exclusively German Bishopric in Bethlehem was ignored and instead the pastor of the German congregation in Jerusalem was promoted to Propst.[41] As Propst he was responsible for coordinating the efforts between the various German mission societies.

VII.
German Protestant Work in Palestine between the Two World Wars[42]

After Germany's defeat in the First World War, German mission work in Palestine experienced a setback. At the same time the sudden interning of German missionaries from Palestine in addition to a stronger national identity caused an awakening within Arab Protestant congregations. The need for indigenization became apparent[43] and the quest for a Christian Palestinian identity and Protestant unity among the different Arab Protestant congregations began to take root before it was interrupted by the Second World War.

VIII.
The Second World War and the Influence of the Lutheran World Federation[44]

The Second World War was a devastating blow to the German Protestant Mission work in Palestine with German mission societies suffering grave financial difficulties as a result of the war. In addition, most of their property in Palestine was placed under British custodianship. The conflict between the Palestinians and the Jews escalated to war in 1948 with catastrophic effects on the work of the Arab Protestant congregations. Sixty five percent of all German mission institutions were located in what came to be the State of Israel. The Schneller and Kaiserwerth institutions lost almost all their property when the institutions were confiscated after the Holocaust as land belonging to the enemy.[45] Later, some compensation was paid by Israel to these institutions enabling Schneller to begin new work in Jordan and Lebanon[46] while Kaiserwerth decided to found a new Talitha Kumi in the West Bank.[47] Many Arab Protestants lost all their property and became refugees.

In response to this situation the National Lutheran Council in the United States and its "Commission on Younger Churches and Orphaned Missions"(CYCOM) decided to send Dr. Edwin Moll to Palestine to study the situation of German mission work and to offer the assistance of the National Lutheran Council. An emergency budget from CYCOM was placed at his disposal. Later he became the representative of the newly established Lutheran World Federation in 1947. It was under Dr. Moll's leadership that restructuring and recognition of all German mission and congregation work in Palestine occurred.[48]

In early 1947, Dr. Moll established a "Provisional Committee of the Palestinian Evangelical Lutheran Church." Two new ideas were emphasized by Dr. Moll namely, Lutheran heritage and the establishment of a unified Lutheran Church. The three German institutions working in Palestine were not from a pure Lutheran background but of a unified Lutheran – Reformed background. The influence of the Lutheran World Federation dominated. For almost one hundred years different Protestant congregations from a German background had existed side-by- side. It was Dr. Moll's wish to unify these congregations into one Church; this was achieved in 1959.[49]

Another result of Dr. Moll's efforts was the opening of the Augusta Victoria Hospital in Jerusalem with the aid of UNRWA(United Nations Relief and Works Agency for Palestinian Refugees in the Near East). An emergency relief program was initiated providing food, shelter, clothing, and medical care. "Next only to the Government and UNRWA, the Lutheran World Federation(Near East Branch) became the third largest employer in the Hashmite Kingdom of Jordan. In the total operation four hundred people were employed."[50]

IX.
The Establishment of the Evangelical Lutheran Church in Jordan

With the help of the Lutheran World Federation and the different German mission institutions a process of consultation and organization began resulting in the establishment of the Evangelical Lutheran Church in Jordan, which was officially recognized by the Jordanian government in May 1959. According to the constitution of the newly formed Church, the different congregations would elect church elders who would then elect representatives for the Synod(the legislative body). The Synod members would in turn elect the members for the Church Council(the executive body). The Synod was headed by a president and the Church Council by a spiritual leader. While the president, from the beginning, had always been an Arab, the spiritual leader was, until 1979, the German Propst.[51] In 1979 the first Arab bishop was elected to succeed the German Propst.[52] Today the Evangelical Lutheran Church in Jordan and the Holy Land is an independent Arab Palestinian Church consisting of six congregation five of whom are in the Occupied Territories(Bethlehem, Beit Jala, Beit Sahour, Jerusalem and Ramallah) and one in Amman, the capital of Jordan.

X.
The Lutheran Church in Palestine Today

The work of the Lutheran Church in Palestine has a distinguished history as it was not connected with or interested in the traditional Holy Sites of Palestine. Rather the Lutheran Church has invested in five main areas

A.
Education

It is highly interesting to note that the first task of the Protestant missionaries who came to Palestine was not to build churches, but to establish schools. Schools thus proceeded churches, and church work was an outgrowth of educational work, not the other way around. Education and the spread of knowledge have been top priorities of the Lutheran Church from the beginning, a fact is related to the Lutheran heritage which underscores the importance of Holy Scripture, enhances its knowledge, encourages its reading and embraces its practice in daily life. Currently, the Evangelical Lutheran Church operates four schools with approximately three thousand pupils in five cities in the Occupied Territories. Indeed educational Christian work in Palestine continues to be greatly needed today.

A look at the political landscape of the Middle East shows that it lacks any logic. The policy of Israel, as well as most of the Arab states, often appears to be irrational, incalculable, and incomprehensible. Yet, religion too often seems to be naïve, fundamentalist and ambiguous. Because of these factors knowledge, training and education are important for the future of Palestinian society in general, as well as for the Christian community in particular. Education is essential for the region as well as for the establishment and nurture of a prosperous and sane society.[53]

B.
Social Work

From the beginning Protestant mission efforts in Palestine focused on social work dealing with orphans, the socially marginalized poor, the sick and refugees. The Church saw her mission as an echo of the mission of her Lord, who was sent to bring Good News to the poor, to proclaim release to the 'captives and recovery of sight. Welfare services alone, however, are not enough. Committed Christians realize today that poverty and oppression are not accidental but are the result of repressive politics that increase the wealth and power of the individual, at the expense of others-the community. It is, therefore, critically important for the Church to work for social justice and to engage herself in building a healthy and well-developed infrastructure in Palestine.[54]

C.
Contextualized Theology

No one denies that the Lutheran experience has focused on a solid understanding of Holy Scripture. For this reason, preaching, Bible studies and exegesis have been crucial elements in the Lutheran experience.

Heretofore, Churches in the Middle East have either recalled the theologies of the Church Fathers, or imported Western theology. The Church has been(and this is part of Palestinian reality) a consuming Church. It is time to develop a Palestinian Christian theology, which reflects our situation and deals with the problems of the Christian communities now. Christianity is not an eternal law, but, a gospel of God who was incarnated in Christ in a certain space and at a certain time. Developing such an incarnated contextualized theology requires ecumenical spirit to face the problems in the region which challenge all the Churches, without exception.[55]

D.
Relationship with the Worldwide Christian Community

Developing a contextualized Palestinian Christian theology is of utmost necessity not only for the local Church, but also for the Universal Church. It is no secret that many Western Christians, especially Protestants, misuse the Bible to fit their own ideology.

The uncritical and historical equating of today's State of Israel with Biblical Israel, theologians guilt over the Holocaust, and Israel's victory over the Arab states has led many Western theologians to mythologize the State of Israel. The other side of this mythologization is the demonization of the Palestinians.[56] The local Palestinian Church has a mission to the Universal Church in underscoring the justice of God as the hermeneutical key in reading and interpreting the Bible, thus becoming the voice of the voiceless.

E.
Dialogue with the Two Other Monotheistic Religions

Christians in Palestine live in a multi-cultural and multi – religious context. They live as a minority among two other majorities(Islam and Judaism). The Christian Church must redefine the concepts of religion giving it new content, as the role of religion is often either ignored and underestimated, or politicized. Religion, if correctly understood, is a positive relationship between God and humans simultaneously forming the basis for all relationships of every person to another and to the environment.[57] In this regard, the position of human beings in religion has to be clarified. A theology of creation can be very important for us in Palestine, where three religions and two nations must coexist. Such a theology holds that every person, irrespective of religion or nationality, is first and foremost human. Dialogue among all people of goodwill is essential for development in the region.[58]

This paper is an attempt to summarize the past and the present of the Evangelical Lutheran Church in Jordan and the Holy Land, describing one hundred and fifty years of history in Palestine.

5.

The Situation of the Palestinian Christian Community in the Holy Land

I can still remember the first time I met with a tourist group and the expression on their faces when they heard that I am a Palestinian Christian.[1] I discovered that they knew little about the Palestinians, and almost nothing about the existence of Palestinian Christians. Their first question to me was, "When did you convert to Christianity?" They assumed that missionaries from the "American midwest" had introduced Christianity to the Holy Land. They were truly astonished to learn that my family has been Christian for hundreds of years, and that the first missionary to come to Bethlehem was Jesus of Nazareth. They were even more bewildered to hear that I am not only a Palestinian Christian, but also an Arab Lutheran pastor at Christmas Lutheran Church in Bethlehem.

Every year during Advent journalists from all over the world flock to "the little town" to write their "Christmas story." The situation of Christians in Palestine in general, and in Bethlehem in particular, has become the focus of media attention in recent years. What is the situation of Palestinian Christians? How do they feel? Is their existence threatened? Do they suffer persecution? What about their future? The following is a brief description of the main characteristics of the Palestinian Christian community, as I see it. As such it is not an objective perception but rather a personal insight.

Christians are Indigenous to the Holy Land

Christianity might seem for many to be a Western phenomenon, but that is a misconception, as Christianity is a West Asian "Palestinian" phenomenon. Jesus Christ was born in Palestine, and it is here that he taught, suffered, was crucified and resurrected. The first Christian communities originated in Palestine. Palestinian Christians thus see themselves as the descendants of these first Jewish and "Gentile" Christians, who were able to survive a turbulent two thousand year history. Christianity was not imported into Palestine. In fact, it is the only "product" that has been successfully "exported" from Palestine to the whole world. In a sense, Christianity is a "Palestinian Trademark." Indeed, Christians were living in Palestine before Muslims arrived on the scene. In the year 2000 Palestinian Christians celebrated two thousand years of continuous history and presence in Palestine, from Pentecost on, without interruption. Christians, therefore, understandably see themselves "at home" in Palestine. Here lie their historical roots. They belong in the fullest sense of the word. Yet the question is: will they be here in the future? There are, unfortunately, serious doubts if Christianity will survive even the 21st century in Palestine. Much will depend on political, economic, and social developments in the region.

Christians at the Holy Sites

For several centuries, Christians constituted the overwhelming majority of the population in Palestine. The shift from being a majority to becoming a minority was one of the results of the Crusades. Not only were the crusaders hostile to local "Palestinian" Christians, but after their defeat the Muslims who followed were not as tolerant towards Christians as previously. As a result of the Crusades, the percentage of Palestinian Christians has decreased steadily. At the beginning of the 20th century thousands of Palestinian Christians from the larger Bethlehem area fled to Latin and South America refusing to be drafted into the Turkish army in preparation for WWI[2]. Another major reason for the decline of Palestinian Christians has to do with the creation of the State of Israel. Thirty five percent of the Christian community in Palestine lost its land and homes in the same year Israel was created, 1948, and became refugees in neighboring Arab countries or in the West. In that epochal year, their percentage in Palestine dropped from 8% to 2.8% just within a few months.[3] Many of those who survived the displacement decided to emigrate because of ongoing political and economic instability in the country. Unfortunately, it was largely those who were educated, capable or well-off financially who were lost by this brain drain. Christianity has disappeared from many Palestinian cities and from almost all Palestinian villages over the centuries but has survived at the holy sites. An examination of where Christians live today in the Holy Land reveals them to be living around those holy sites. In the West Bank[4], they are mainly clustered in and around Bethlehem and Jerusalem, whereas in Israel, they are to be found mainly in Nazareth and the Galilee. Christians have always felt responsible for protecting and defending these churches and sites, but they also felt safe there in times of persecution and oppression; although most of the keys to the holy sites are not in the hands of Palestinian Christians but are kept by expatriate Christians, Western religious Orders or even the hands of Muslim key keepers. The siege of the Church of the Nativity in the year 2002[5] might have some lasting impact on the Palestinian Christian community in that was commonly believed that the holy sites had until then always provided safe refuge but for the first time a haven was violated and shattered.

A Mosaic of Many Denominations

The existence of various denominations and churches is typical of Christianity in Palestine.[6] From a Euro-centric perspective, the first Church schism occurred with the Reformation. But the history of Eastern Christianity reveals that pluralism was a main feature of the Christian community as early as the first century, for the simple reason that the Gospel of Jesus Christ was contrary to faiths based on laws and always eager to relate to indigenous cultures and contexts. A number of so-called "national churches" were established in the first five centuries: The Greek Orthodox Church, The Coptic Orthodox Church, the Syrian Orthodox(Jacobite) Church, the Armenian Orthodox(Gregorian) Church, the Apostolic Church of the East(Nestorian) and others.[7] As a result of contacts with the Roman Catholic Church during the Middle Ages, a variety of these "united churches" were also established in Palestine.[8] These churches maintained their Eastern rite in tradition and liturgy while at the same time recognizing the primacy of the Pope. During the nineteenth century, missionary efforts, mainly among the Oriental Churches resulted in the establishment of new churches: the Roman Catholic(Latin)[9] Church, the Evangelical Lutheran Church in Jordan and the Holy Land[10] and the Anglican Church. Today, there are almost thirty nine different Christian denominations in Jerusalem. This diversity of denominations is unique. It is simultaneously also a blessing and a curse, for therein lies the strength but also the weakness of the Palestinian Christian community, a sign of multifaceted richness while at the same time a source of conflict and adversity.

A Religious Minority

Christians over the course of time have become a minority in Palestine and Israel. Today, the percentage of Christians in Israel and Palestine is less than two percent of the total population. There are around one hundred twenty thousand Palestinian Christians in Israel(as well as approximately three thousand Messianic Jews) and fifty thousand in the West Bank and Gaza Strip. In the diaspora, there are some three hundred thousand Palestinian Christians who are scattered over the globe. In all, there are about five hundred thousand Palestinian Christians, who comprise seven – ten percent of the total Palestinian population.

Due to emigration, however, the majority of Palestinian Christians live in the diaspora. Socio-economic factors and the political situation continue to be the main contributory reasons for this population drain. The collapse of the "Peace Process," the Intifadas, as well as the reintroduction of Israeli military rule in the West Bank and Gaza are forcing ever greater numbers of Christians to emigrate in order to seek a better future for their children. If this trend continues, the Holy Land will soon be turned into a theme park of Christian history rather than a site of living Christian witness and service.

An Engaged Minority

Christians in Palestine are a minority. Living as a minority is not always easy. It leads some Christians to develop a fear of the majority. Others assume a superiority complex; a feeling of being culturally above Muslims. Still others assume an inferiority complex which is often expressed by a strong sense of nationalism. These Christians feel they have to prove their loyalty to the "cause" thus becoming more royal than the King. But seldom have Palestinian Christians been marginalized or a self-centered group. They have remained an engaged minority. Being a minority was and is a statement of fact regarding their quantity, not their quality. Their modern contribution to the fields of social, diaconal and educational work should not be underestimated.¹¹ Of the 2200+ schools in the West Bank and Gaza, sixty two are Christian schools, mainly Catholic and Lutheran. They belong to an advanced group of schools in Palestine and are open for Christians and Muslims alike. Of twenty four hospitals, nine are Christian which serve a Muslim majority. Christians today operate ten major social institutions, twelve rehabilitation centers, seven old-age homes and twelve orphanages. European Churches and Church-related institutions fund, to a large extent, over half of the human rights centers in Israel and Palestine. Palestinian Christians were and are still highly vocal when it comes to advocating justice, developing non-violent resistance[12] and promoting reconciliation. There is no sign whatsoever that this role assumed by Christians is decreasing. On the contrary, in the last ten years most of these Christian service centers have been renovated and/or enlarged and several new centers opened.

Arab Christians

Although Christians in Palestine are a minority, they are not an ethnic but a religious minority. They understand themselves to be part and parcel of Arab civilization and culture. This should not be taken for granted. In neighboring countries, Christians often do not understand themselves to be Arabs. Lebanese Maronite Christians for instance like to think of themselves as being Phoenicians, Coptic Christians as being descendents of the Pharaohs, Iraqi Christians as being "Assyrians," etc. The fact that Palestinian Christians today understand themselves to be Arabs does not mean that historically speaking they always have been Arabs. In the West, the term "Arab" is equated with "Muslim." This is a misconception of both Middle Eastern history and Christianity, since Arab Christians are neither a new invention nor a Western product. The evangelist Luke reports in

Acts 2:11 that Arabs were present at the first feast of Pentecost. Thus, Arab Christians were among the first Christians. It is, unsurprising, therefore, that the Apostle Paul retired to Arabia immediately after his conversion(Gal 1:17). Arab Christianity[13] is consequently older than Islam itself. Christians in Palestine were originally Aramaic-speaking Christians(like Jesus), who were forced to become "Orthodox" in the post- Constantinian era and arabized in the course of history, especially after the Muslim conquest of Palestine in 637 AD. As early as the 9th century at the Mar Saba Monastery, close to Bethlehem, the first Arabic Summa Theologica was developed.[14] During the 19th century, Arab Christians played a pivotal role in shaking the Arab world out of its deep medieval sleep, promoting the renaissance of Arab culture and language, and introducing modern ideas and values to the Arab world.[15]

Part and Parcel of the Palestinian People

Christians in Palestine share the same fears and hopes as their Muslim neighbors. The Zionist movement, the politics of the British Mandate, the refugee experience and the ongoing Israeli occupation have affected Muslims and Christians alike. This shared suffering means that Muslims and Christians have the same dreams and hopes and work for common goals. Throughout modern history Christians and Muslims in Palestine have worked together against "Muslim" Ottoman rule, against the "Christian" British Mandate and, as well, against the "Jewish" Israeli occupation.

In addition, Christians played a leading role in the secular Palestinian Liberation Organization that was established in 1964. George Habash, former Chairperson of the Popular Front for the Liberation of Palestine(P.F.L.P) and Naef Hawatmeh, Chairperson of the

Democratic Front for the Liberation of Palestine (D.F.L.P) are both Christians. Within the Palestinian Authority itself, Christians hold key positions. The mayors of Ramallah, Bethlehem, Beit Sahour and Beit Jala are Christian, as are the mayors of smaller villages like Taybeh, Zababdeh, Bir Zeit, Rafiddiyye and others. President Arafat was married to a Christian. He also had Christians among his top aids, including Ramzi Khoury (Director of the President's Office), Nabil Abu Rudeineh (Media Advisor and Spokesperson), Jirius Attrash (General Director, Bethlehem Office) and Sami Mussalam (General Director, Jericho Office). Christians hold key governmental posts too and there are usually two Christian cabinet ministers at any time. The PLO Executive Committee includes several Christians. Of the eighty two seats of the Palestinian National Council (Parliament), six are, by law, reserved for Christians. Yet, many Christians find themselves today in a crisis: the PLO itself is in crisis. It did not deliver what it promised to deliver - a secular and democratic Palestinian state (or at least a state of mind) and society is in a state of despair which is expressed by a growing fundamentalist movement, and by an opportunistic and incapable Palestinian Authority. Many Palestinian Christians feel that this cannot be what they were ready to die and live for and are growing increasingly disinterested politically, but are not necessarily socially disengaged. Yet they are disillusioned.

A Bridge between the Arab World and the Western World

Just as Palestinian Christians understand themselves to be an inseparable part of the Arab Islamic world, they also see themselves as being an inseparable part of a worldwide Christian Church. They belong to both the Arab world and the universal Church. For centuries, belonging to two worlds has constituted a great challenge; one which has not always been easy to resolve. Often it seemed as though Palestinian Christians were caught in between. They were sometimes misunderstood and even betrayed by both sides. During the middle Ages they were persecuted on one hand by the Crusaders because of their Eastern Church affiliation, and on the other hand by some fanatic Muslim Caliphs. Yet they were frequently also able to profit from this double belonging. They were able to obtain help from their brothers and sisters in the West, and at the same time, promote understanding for the Arab world. In short, they often functioned as transcenders of borders and as bridge builders.

A Persecuted Community?

Is the Christian community in the Holy Land persecuted? If persecution means a systematic policy of discrimination because of beliefs, then the answer is definitely: no. Neither in Israel nor in Palestine are Christians persecuted for their faith in Christ. But in both contexts Christians are facing difficult times. In the Occupied Palestinian Territories, Christians, like Muslims, are suffering under Israeli occupation. They cannot travel and move freely, thousands spend months and years in Israeli prisons for their political convictions, some are deported and many thousands have been displaced from their ancestral homes and villages. For the Israelis, Christians in the Palestinian territories are primarily Palestinians and they are treated as such.[16] In Israel, Palestinian Christians are second-class citizens, since they are viewed primarily as Arabs, [17] and as such they are discriminated against. They are prohibited by law as non-Jews from leasing or buying land from the Jewish National Fund and they receive only two percent of the budget of the Ministry of Religious Affairs, despite the fact that Muslims, Christians and Druze constitute over twenty percent of the population. As well, under the 1967

Protection of Holy Sites law, the Israeli government has recognized only Jewish holy places, thereby denying government funding for the preservation of Christian or Muslim religious sites. Additionally, the Law of Return guarantees immediate and automatic citizenship to Jewish immigrants regardless of nationality, but forbids native Christians and Muslims from returning who were forced to flee during the 1948 and 1967 wars.

In the Palestinian autonomous areas, Christians enjoy the protection of the Palestinian Authority but, at the same time, they are concerned because of the weakness of democratic structures and laws, where the minority accepts the rule of the majority, where the majority protects the rights of the minority and where conflicts are solved by adhering to one law. In Israel Palestinian Arab Christians are recognized as a community but Messianic Jews,[18] as such, are not. The State of Israel does not recognize Jews who believe in Christ as their Messiah as Jews. They have to choose between being Jewish or Christian but not a "Messianic Jew." It is important to note that both the reform and conservative Jewish movements, the two major American Jewish movements, are also not recognized in Israel, since the Orthodox Rabbinate has a monopoly over deciding of who is a Jew and it alone sets the criteria and performs all legal Jewish rites (marriages' burials etc.).

A Community Sailing Through Troubled Waters

The Palestinian Christian community is a community that is greatly affected by what happens in the Middle East and even in many other parts of the world. The symbol of the Church as a ship sailing through troubled waters is a perfect description of the Palestinian Christian community. The "clash of civilizations" presents a challenge for a community one of whose most important characteristics is its existence within two civilizations. Osama bin Laden's videos, where he described Christians as infidels, presented a threat to a community which sees itself as part and parcel of an Arab Islamic world. George W. Bush's words about the new crusades were no less threatening to a community who suffered under the crusaders in the Middle Ages and which continues to live within a Muslim context that is still traumatized by that terrible event. Zionist reading of the Bible is another major threat that turns the Good News into bad news for Palestinian Christians by siding with Israel and theologically and financially supporting its settlement activities. It takes enormous effort for a small community, such as the Palestinian Christian community, to resist the many different groups who try to pirate this ship and lead it to their own ends. In this sense, several debates, reports and articles published by the Israeli government,[19] or the Christian Coalition on the persecution of Christians in Palestine are but attempts to instrumentalize the fate of the Palestinian Christian community for their own political gain; the Israeli government to undermine the Palestinian Authority and to portray it as an anti Christian government, and the Christian Coalition as part of its strategy to strengthen the "identity" of its followers by focusing on a strong Muslim and anti-Christian enemy. The same is true also for fundamentalist Muslim groups who need a scapegoat for their own failures. It requires great skill to keep developing an open and dynamic identity in the face of these very different and conflicting, closed, and static identities. Skill and talent is needed to sail through these troubled waters without losing one's way.

Christians in a Context of Uncertainty and Instability

Today, Palestine and Israel are experiencing a state of uncertainty and political, social, economic as well as religious instability. All of these changes are affecting Christians. Some feel afraid and some lose their hope in Palestine while others see no future for their children in the region. Yet others firmly believe that they are here to stay and to be a witness for an open, active and dynamic community in the birthplace of Christianity. I believe that we, as Christians in Palestine, are not spectators but actors in our history. We cannot, as living stones, choose but to engage ourselves, get our hands dirty, and become involved in the changes occurring around us so that a state emphasizing the best for the public and its welfare emerges. At a time when despair and hopelessness are growing, our role as Palestinian Christians can be best summed up in the words of Martin Luther, "Even if I knew that the world is coming to an end tomorrow, today I would go out to my garden and plant an apple tree." Or as we say in Palestine, in a more contextual way, "Plant an olive tree." Because only then will our children, after tomorrow, have shade to play under, have olive oil to eat, olive oil with which to heal their wounds, and olive branches to wave as a sign for the peace to come.

6.

The Revolution in the Arab World
Towards a Public Theology of Liberation

I have chosen not to use the name "the Arab spring "in the title of this article, a word first used in 2005 by the Lebanese thinker of Palestinian origin, Samir Kassir, because it has a positive connotation and qualification that I cannot except as a given. Rather, I would like to look on what is happening in the Arab world today solely in a dialectical way. This Arab revolution, I firmly believe, is open-ended and simultaneously holds both a promise of liberation and an illusion of a new era.

Where Do We Come From?

To know where we stand today, we need to see where we come from, hoping that this will help us understand where we are heading. If we look back at the history of the Middle East, in the last one hundred years, we see that there were six decisive moments that shaped the history of the last half century in our region and which led to this moment.

1. One cannot understand what is happening today in the Middle East unless we begin with the First World War. With the defeat of the German-Turkish alliance, the Ottoman Empire was dissolved. The Arabs, who had been given the promise of national liberation

by the British, were faced with the stark reality that those promises were nothing but lip service. Instead, new countries with new boundaries were created in the Fertile Crescent and were placed under the mandate of the victorious powers, namely England and France, while a new promise was made by Lord Balfour of England to create a national homeland for the Jewish people in Palestine. This was the one promise made at the time of the First World War that was fulfilled. The promises made in and around the Great War were thus one of history's great illusions.

2. We must remember that all of the leaders who are being ousted from the Middle East today came to power through national revolutions; they were the young revolutionaries forty years ago. At that time they brought with them several promises: the promise of independence from the "Colonial West"; the promise of unity for the Arab world; and the promise of socialism that the ordinary person would have a better life. This was true for Ghadafi, Nasser and Mubarak after him, Borkeba who preceded Bin Ali in Tunisia, Assad, the father, etc. These national revolutions were the second decisive moment.

3. The third decisive moment occurred in 1967 when all of these leaders were defeated by Israel in war. That was the first time when the people of the Arab world encountered the illusion of the revolution. Great revolutions ended in humiliating defeat, and that defeat and a sense of being defeated has shaped the last forty years in the Arab world.

4. The fourth decisive moment followed shortly after the war of 1967 with the discovery of oil as a political weapon and the emergence of the so-called petro-dollar. For the first time in the history of our region the center of gravity moved from the so-called Fertile Crescent to the Arabian Peninsula and to the Gulf region.

The influence of countries like Saudi Arabia and Qatar slowly but surely became highly visible and a desert culture started invading the landscape of the Middle East.

5. The fifth decisive moment took place in 1979 when another revolution, this time an Islamic one, burst on to the scene. This Islamic revolution's aim was to oust a dictator, the "Shah." Basically, Iran had its equivalent of the current revolution, in the Middle East thirty years ago, when a dictator was removed from power and the promise of a divine state was proclaimed far and wide.

6. And last but not least, the sixth decisive moment in the Middle East occurred in 1982. I am not referring here to the war in Lebanon. I am talking about another revolution- one which took place under the radar screen. Yet for me this may have been the most important of the revolutions. The year 1982 was the year of the electronic revolution when the world moved from typewriters to computers. This revolution was not about typing; it literally changed the worldwide economy and it changed the global way of education. This revolution was the only revolution that did not make a stop in the Arab world; it simply bypassed our region. The United Nations "Arab Human Development Report(2003)" shows in chart form how development in the Arab world up until 1982 was somewhat parallel with the rest of the world. Beginning in 1982, however, the Arab world began sliding downwards because its governments did not recognize the importance of the electronic revolution and thus they missed the future.

This is where we have come from in the last one hundred years. During that century new generations were born. The old generation "who left Egypt" throughout the six aforementioned revolutions "died in the desert," and did not live to see "the Promised Land." But the new generation looked around and what did it see?

Where Are We Now?

1. The new Arab generation saw nothing left from those national revolutions; nothing but security states that were making their lives miserable. They also saw that all of the nation states of the region were run as private businesses. Power was handed from father to son even in the most socialist oriented countries; the wife of "X" controlled seventy percent of the economy; the brother of "Y" ran a good portion of state businesses and so on. This new generation "born in the desert" gradually grew disillusioned. One month before the latest revolution started we, at the Diyar Consortium, conducted a study on the "Cultural Practices of the Palestinian Youth" and discovered that only eighteen percent of young people in Palestine were connected to a political party. The majority did not even want to hear the word "politics." They were and are disillusioned.

2. This new generation "born in the desert" had from childhood heard about Israel being the enemy, yet they felt that the defeat of 1967 was on-going. The rhetoric they were exposed to said that all the Arab countries were working hard to free Palestine, but young people experienced the second intifada, they watched the war on Gaza, and they felt humiliated. It is not easy for young people to feel both humiliated and hopeless.

3. This new generation "born in the desert" opened their eyes and found a polarized society. They turned on their televisions and all they saw were clerics preaching or belly dancers and nothing in between. It is tough to live in such a polarized society where there is little if anything in the middle. Interestingly, in the study Diyar did on "Cultural Practices of the Palestinian Youth" there was a question about religion. The responses to this question were

also polarized. Young people in Palestine were either totally for religion or totally against religion.

Yet that which is common to all of this new generation is that they have no problem in "worshiping the golden calf," or what is today called, consumerism. The single event at our center in Bethlehem that attracted the largest number of young people was the screening of an Egyptian film entitled "Omar wa Salma" starring the young Egyptian actor Tamer Hosni, who is the superstar of the youth of the Arab world. This film was the only event where more than two thousand people poured into the streets and closed the old city of Bethlehem because they wanted to view it. I told myself that I had to see what the film was all about! Only to discover that it was about the new Arab consumer society. The film showed young people cars, mobiles, iPads, girls and boys in open relationships, etc... In short, all of the hallmarks of a consumer society about which they dream but do not have; the promise of the illusion.

4. This new generation "born in the desert" has an unemployment rate of 25%. It is a generation "born in the desert" but raised with television satellite dishes sprouting from the tops of their parents' homes with a choice of more than a thousand channels; a generation that spends three hours a day on average on Facebook. It has its morning devotions with Facebook and before it goes to bed a good night kiss is given to the social networking website. Facebook is their liturgy and they take it far more seriously than Christians who read their Bibles. What this generation sees on these thousand plus television channels and via Facebook raises its expectations higher and higher; they see a world of endless possibilities and, quite naturally, they want to tap into it.

Born in the desert, the road to the Promised Land for this new generation is possible only virtually. The feeling has thus grown even stronger among young people that they are "stuck in the desert." The desert is a very rough place and the heat can become unbearable and, as a result, things started to boil. A silent peoples' revolution began to simmer because the frustrations of young people were steadily growing, and all that was needed for someone to set things on fire, which a young man in Tunisia did. After him, the Middle East started shaking. A tsunami swept through the Arab world beginning in Tunisia followed by Egypt, Libya, Yemen, Bahrain, Syria, Jordan, and Morocco with perhaps others to follow, with the exception of Palestine.

For the first time, we in Palestine had the luxury of not being on international television news but to sit and watch. For a change, this was really good. We were able, at least, to catch our breath. But the upheavals changes in the Arab world will have their impact on Palestine. Currently these changes are forcing Fatah and Hamas to re-position themselves, waiting for the dust of the revolution to clear before they take a more steady position.

The Liberation:
A Promise and / or an Illusion?

The revolutions in the Middle East are both a promise and an illusion and are thus in a dialectical relationship.

The promise: We see a new era evolving in the Middle East, after which the region will never be the same. And yet, we remain and live with the same people and the same infrastructures. For the first time in forty years there is a new hope that one can feel. It is compatible with Obama's "Yes We Can"; and young people in Middle East today are saying just that. This is the promise. The illusion, however, is that the promise is easier said than done because it still requires hard work. We have seen how Obama's promises are fading into the sunset. Are young people in the Arab world today ready for a long and thorny process?

The promise: It is the young people of the Middle East, who are not politicized who are pouring into the streets just like their counterparts in Europe. Yet the illusion is that without military regimes nothing would have been possible. It is the military in Egypt, who seems to behave "neutrally," who was in favor of change. It was Western military strikes in Libya that made change there possible and it is the military in Syria who is keeping leaders in place and in power.

We have the promise of new emerging political parties. We watched the elections in Tunisia with several parties competing. Such promise is great for it is needed; an alternative to the ruling parties on the one hand and to the Islamists in opposition on the other. Yet, the illusion is that the Islamists are thus far more organized. Perhaps the most important and decisive question in the Middle East today is not whether we are headed towards a new Islamic era but rather what type of Islamic era? Which Islamic model will prevail? The Saudi, the Turkish, the one in Qatar? In all likelihood several Islamic models will compete with each other to prove who is more authentic and who is more successful.

It seems to me that a kind of neo-conservative Islam is on the horizon which is religiously conservative but very much consumer-oriented and consequently economically neo-liberal. It can satisfy to some extent, some of the "needs" of the people of the Middle East which fits very well with Western interests and a consumer market of 350 million Arabs.

The Middle East appears to be undergoing radical change. Nevertheless, actual change is still limited.

We are also experiencing a new regrouping between those countries who have a monarchy and oil reserves and those who are experiencing revolutions but have only scarce resources; between those who can satisfy the consumer demands and needs of their peoples but not necessarily their rights, and those who might be able to satisfy the rights of their people but not their needs. The rift seems to be between the desert Arab states versus the states of the Fertile Crescent. This is a frightening situation.

There is a real danger at present of the Middle East being dismantled and "Balkanized." Sudan has been divided into two, Iraq might be divided into three sectors, Syria might be divided into three, Lebanon continues to be turned into two like Palestine (the West Bank vs. Gaza) and we do not know how many "Libyas" and "Yemens" will yet emerge. We may in fact be witnessing the fracturing of the whole Middle East.

The region may also be split between Shiities and Suni Muslims. Such a scenario might push the region into a new wave of militarisation that would exploit the resources of the region and would only benefit the war lords and the global weapons trade.

The promise: For the first time in the Arab world we have a revolution that is largely peaceful. What happened in Tunisia and in Egypt was much like what happened in Leipzig in Germany, when candles brought down the Wall. Yet, Libya, Syria and maybe other countries, are very bloody scenes. The revolution should not be underestimated, but at the same time it should not be overestimated. As someone who believes more in process than in revolution, the promise of this revolution can only be realized if it occurs at the beginning of the process. The revolution is but the start, and the process has yet to deliver. The work is not behind us, it has just begun.

Towards a Public Theology of Liberation

It is very difficult to predict where we are heading; it is perhaps easier to say where we should be heading. For the promise to yield fruit we need to remember where we came from and what still needs to be done. One of the most crucial and urgent steps is to develop a public theology of liberation for the Arab world today. To that end, I see seven components for such a theology:

1. Liberation is what the Arab peoples are longing for, and it is a central theme in the Bible. Liberation from oppression as well as liberation from religious laws. In this sense theologians in the Arab world have a unique calling to articulate and help liberate their peoples from dictatorships and oppressive regimes as well as ensuring that the new Islamist parties will not oppress peoples with new religious laws that violate human rights.

2. For liberation to be true, we need new legislation and modern constitutions. After Moses was able to get rid of Pharaoh, and went through the Red Sea, when the waters parted, it was the law, the Ten Commandments, that was given to him. A new constitution was needed, and everyone was under the rule of law, including Moses which is why he was not able to enter the Promised Land, because he too was under the law. Today this is called accountability.

3. For the liberation to yield fruit, the region has to move from a one-party system which has been the norm in the Arab world into a multi-party system where Islamists are also included. There are a few key questions that need to be dealt with in this regard.

One of them is the relationship between religion and state. Whatever the solution or the formula, there is no way forward but to establish a civil society. In fact, if we ponder why the revolution in Egypt was relatively peaceful compared with Syria; the answer is that there is a strong civil society in Egypt while there is almost no civil society in Syria. And if we ask why the annahda Islamic party in Tunisia is more progressive than the one in Libya, the answer lies in Tunisian civil society. The work that has been carried out by numerous non-governmental organizations over the last twenty years is a building block in the process of establishing civil societies although people have not always been able to recognize that contribution.

4. The Arab world which is threatened by Balkanization and fragmentation is in need of a new and inclusive vision. Jerusalem at Pentecost, where different identities represented by different languages made communication possible through the Spirit, could function as a paradigm today. The Arab world is in need of a new spirit that is based on the notion of citizenship. Citizenship is critical because it provides unity throughout great much diversity we have in the Middle East, including religious, ethnic and national differences.

5. For the liberation to bring forth fruit, we need to solve the Palestinian question. Without solving this conflict there will be no possibility for the Middle East to focus on development. We cannot focus on development, we cannot focus on economy, we cannot focus on the future unless this conflict is resolved once and for all; otherwise, it will continue to pull down the whole region. When it comes to Palestine, theology has unfortunately been part of the problem rather than part of the solution. This is true not only for Christian Zionist theology, but also for the liberal theology of the Judeo-Christian dialogue that left the occupation of Palestine un-

der the radar screen of dialogue. Liberation of the Palestinian Arabs from the Israeli occupation and the liberation of Arab nations from dictatorships are two sides of one coin.

6. Liberation has to meet the expectations of young people and future generations. What are those expectations? Young people desperately need education with an illiteracy rate of 35.6% in the Arab world today(compared to 18% globally). They need jobs in a region with the world's lowest employment rate and where in the next ten years over fifty million new jobs need to be created. Who will create these? Young adults want jobs, they want space to move freely, they yearn to be able to express themselves without fearing the security state; they want to have life and to have it abundantly. None of this is possible without a new unifying vision for the-region-at large and for each country separately. The people of the Middle East have to take responsibility for building their future together.

7. We are in urgent need of a prophetic theology if liberation is to be real and not an illusion. No one is a spectator, we are all actors. The Arab people are actors and they have proven that. The governments of the Middle East are actors and what they do is important. The US is an actor; Europe is an actor; and Turkey, Iran & Israel are actors. We feel, however, that there are conflicting interests between the values the actors say they espouse such as democracy, human rights, development, etc… and the "real politics" of oil, the global weapons trade and markets. The interests of the Western countries in oil, the support they have given over the decades to Arab dictators, as long as they are in power, and their sudden turn against them once they start to wavier, are signs of this real politics of oil, weapons, and markets and has little to do with human rights or democracy. Prophetic theology must point to these double standards and this inconsistency between what

countries preach and what they end up doing. Prophetic theology should ensure that the hypocrisy of these countries is revealed and dealt with in the international community.

When we look at the revolutions of the Arab world we continue to be torn between the promise and the illusion. Yet the only option we have is to assume responsibility, to develop a "Public Theology of Liberation for the Arab World" and to become ever more active in instigating a real process of change from within.

7.
Human Rights in the Middle East and North Africa:

The Situation of the Christians

The Situation of Christians in the Middle East today within the context of the Arab Spring has become an important issue on the agendas of Human rights organizations as well as Christian mission agencies. I would like to start by putting the whole question in context. As a contextual theologian this is how I usually work. In a second step I will highlight the potential role of Christians in the Middle East today?

The Context

1. Are Christians in the Middle East a minority? This is a greatly debated question! Perhaps for people in Europe it appears that Christians are a minority, but for Christians in the Middle East it is not so very clear. In the West when people talk about a minority, it usually refers to a racial minority: people who come from a different culture, who usually speak a different language, and often have different customs. But Christians in the Middle East are part and parcel of the Middle Eastern society. They speak the same language, have the same customs and share almost everything except religion. So Christians in the Middle East a minority? Many Christians say, no, we are not a minority. The Christians

of the Middle East are not immigrants who came from the West. They have been present in the region before the coming of Islam. Calling Christians a minority is akin to discriminating against them. The more we use the term minority for Christians the more we weaken them. We then revert to sectarian language, and when it comes to sectarian language Christians are on the weaker end. This is why many of the Christians in the Middle East are fighting against the use of the term minority to refer to them.

2. When we talk about the Arab spring we usually forget Israel. Yet we should not leave Israel out of the Middle Eastern equation. Why? Because a look at most of the dictators in the Arab world shows that they came to power almost at the same time as the start of the start of the Israeli occupation. Arab dictatorships and the Israeli occupation are two side of the coin. I know this is not the way people in the West are used to seeing things; they think the Arab countries have dictators and Israel is a democracy. Israel might be democratic to some extent and to some of its citizens within Israel, but when it comes to the West Bank, Israel is according to International Law a military occupation. And all the symptoms of dictatorship in the Arab world are found in the Israel security state: corruption, the oppression of people, inequality; everything that is true of the Arab countries is found in the Israeli occupation. For me we cannot and should not separate the whole issue of occupation from the Arab spring, because, in fact, there can be no spring in the Arab world without ending the Israeli occupation. This is a critical point. If you look at our situation, even if we eventually have democracy throughout the Arab world and the Israeli Palestinian problem still exists, the region as a whole can't focus on development and the future because it is too busy with this pressing conflict. Israel claims that the situation of Christians in Israel is better than in the West Bank and is better than that which exists in the Arab states. But this is a myth!

3. I'm also hesitant to talk about Christian persecution in the Middle East, as the word persecution is one that I would not use because I don't think that in the majority of the Arab world Christians are persecuted as such. I think we have to look at the whole context; and the whole context is basically that in the entire Arab world including Israel, the West Bank and Gaza, there is no democracy, there are no democratic structures, and there is a week civil society. Yes, it is true that Christians don't have complete freedom of religion. But remember we are living in a context where we do not have freedom-full stop!!! Not only freedom of religion; I mean there is no freedom. In that sense there are Muslims Shiites oppressed by Sunni Muslims, or Sunni Muslims oppressed by Alawites. Persecution means that Christians are oppressed systematically because of their belief in Jesus Christ. I doubt that this is the case anywhere in the Arab world or in Israel.

4. There are some Christians in the Middle East who are running to the West, calling for them to come and protect Arab Christians. There are two kinds of protection myths in the Arab world. The first is that which I just mentioned, the idea of Western countries coming to protect us. I don't believe in that since history shows me exactly the opposite! History tells me that it has often been the Western world that let Arab Christians down. I remember reading a letter by an Armenian in 1914, asking the Germans how they could keep silent when so many Armenians were being massacred!? The answer at the time was very straight forward, the political interests of Germany were far more important than the future of the Armenians, so the Armenian correspondent felt that the Germans had let him and his people down. Think of all the promises that Britain gave to the Arabs if they rebelled against the Ottomans. Yet the only promise that was kept was that Israel would have a national homeland. Or think of Saudi Arabia. I always tell Westerners I will start believing you once you go to Sau-

di Arabia and ask the Saudis why they don't allow the building of churches?! But oil is more important than the status of Christians. So please don't come to us and say we want to protect you, because the West has always protected its own interests. Another good example is Iraq. Once George W. Bush brought democracy to Iraq, courtesy of a war, half of the Christians left the country. And that was due to President Bush Jr., who was closely affiliated with the Christians Right. Thus I always tell our people not to fall into the trap of this Western myth. Yet back home we Christians don't want to be protected by Muslims either. There are some Muslim brothers who sometimes say, "We will protect you" to which, I say, I don't want that protection. The protection we are actually fighting for is the protection of a legal system which is the only protection that should be allowed. The laws of a country should be the sole force protecting everyone not only Christians. This is why, for me, the rights of Christians cannot simply be separated from human rights. If we protect human rights we are automatically protecting the rights of Christians. We are not asking for special rights as that would actually be against the concept of human rights for all.

5. We live in a region that is not poor but has poor policies and these are two distinctive things. We live in a context where every year the region spends 1 trillion dollars on weapons. The Middle East is the largest importer of weapons worldwide. In the last ten years 10 trillion dollars were spent on weapons. Who is benefiting from all of this?! Certainly not the people of the region. And the horrendous thing is that most of the time these governments use these weapons against their own people! Except for Israel, and Israel is part of the equation. As long as Israel receives all of its "toys" for free, people in the region think they that they have to spend more to keep up with Israel, so Israel is basically providing incentives for the region to buy even more weaponry. This is poor policy!

One trillion dollars and yet the Middle East have the highest illiteracy rate some 35.6% in the world. If so much money is spent on weapons there is obviously not enough to focus on education. The average illiteracy rate worldwide is approximately 18% and the Middle East has double that percentage. The same is true for unemployment. All of this is a vicious circle; and all of it has to do with context. In the next eight years our region has to generate a staggering fifty million new job opportunities to meet population growth. The challenge for any government elected now is not the election, as elections are easily won, but the challenge is how to create jobs for people. If people are illiterate and unemployed and living under the mantle of a security state, there is no future for Christians. Which means the future of Christians can only be secured if we secure the development of the region as such.

The Role of the Christians in the Middle East

This is a bleak picture. What can we do as Christians? I realize that some Arab Christians when faced with such dismal statistics see no future, and say, "Let's go somewhere else!" Other Christians think that the answer is to create a safe haven where they can sing nice Christian songs, but they retreat from society. I am of the opinion that the only alternative we have as Christians in the Middle East is to engage with society, not emigrate and not withdraw to a safe subculture. There are five ways as Christians that we can be engaged with society. And it is highly important for Christians to be engaged because perhaps no one else can play this particular and vital role.

1. Christians can help develop a unifying vision for the region. This is immensely critical. Our forefathers did it on Pentecost where

all the subcultures of the Middle East at that time gathered in Jerusalem which meant real confusion! The whole image of Pentecost was that true communication was possible between different subcultures because of and through the Holy Spirit who was the unifying vision. Likewise in the 19th century Christians also developed a unifying version in response to the many Christians who were massacred in 1860 in Lebanon by the Druze. Our Christian forefathers, especially the Protestants, instead of calling for revenge, against the Druze, developed the notion of Arab nationalism as a way to bring Christians and Muslims together. Admittedly, in the end it didn't work but, at that time, it was pivotal. They were able to develop a unifying vision. I feel that today a shared vision for the region is absolutely imperative because we are afraid that our region will be Balkanized. There used to be one Sudan, now we have two, there used to be one Iraq now we may end up with three. And no one is certain what will happen with Syria! The West Bank and Gaza Strip used to be thought of as one state, now we have two states although neither is actually a state but each likes to think of themselves as states. What I see taking place is a process of Balkanization, and that which is lacking is a joint vision. The Bible says: "Without a vision, people are just like a horse that will go astray." As Christians we have to engage in providing a unifying vision, not a sectarian vision but a unifying vision.

2. What is Christianity without the concept of freedom? The Old Testament starts with: "Let my people go," and in the New Testament Jesus says, "I came as a savior" which means a liberator to bring freedom. As Christians I think it is crucial to see in the so-called Arab spring the quest for freedom; freedom from tyranny, freedom from occupation, but also, and this is important for us as Lutherans, freedom from Shariaa'; freedom from the tyranny of religious laws. Vis-`a-vis freedom I think we have something to

contribute, because sometimes I think that the Arab world today stands where Europeans stood before the Reformation, and if it were not for Luther who insisted on freedom from from Church law, from Church tradition, there would be no innovation today and we would probably still be in the Middle Ages.

3. There can be no compromise on the issue of equality, no compromise whatsoever. Israelis shall never have more rights than Palestinians, Muslims cannot have more rights than Christians; equality is not a religious value but a human rights value that in no way should be compromised. And we need to find ways to keep emphasizing this issue. There is also the concept of citizenship. If you follow what's happening in the Arab world, there is a great deal of attention given to the issue of citizenship, Why citizenship? Because citizenship is connected to equality. We want to emphasize that we are all citizens of one country with the same rights and same obligations. This is exceedingly important and is also a part of our Christian heritage.

4. There cannot be a spring in the Arab world if there is no spring in the Church. As a Church we can't preach to the Arab world if we churches are part of the system. Again, this is part of our tradition of reformation. I believe that when Martin Luther spoke about Ecclesia Semper Reformanda, the Church that always has to be reformed, ongoing reformation, we can't expect the state to be transformative if our Church structures remain so old-fashioned. I thought it was great, for example, when young Egyptians in the streets stopped listening to Pope Shenouda who was backing Mubarak. That was an example of Ecclesia Semper Reformanda. It was breaking the whole notion that we have a Patriarch and a Pharaoh and he says where to go and we all follow without thinking. There were young people who said, "Wait-let's think about that." I believe this is highly significant and is why reforming

the Churches in the Middle East for me is a critical element in reforming society.

5. The Arab spring is not a matter of a mere three months. Anyone who thinks that the Arab spring will last three months, to be followed by summer and everything will bloom and be sunny is not realistic. For me spring is a process and it is a long process. We can only have a saying in this process, however, if we engage. Other people will jump on that train as we saw with the Islamists, and so, in this process, we need to be engaged, we need to provide a functioning model exemplifying the values about which we are talking. The Arab spring is a process, a long process, and we only have a say if we are part of such a process.

I will conclude with an image of this process at Diyar where we have a female soccer team as women's sports are a very important part of our ministry. Our team is comprised of Muslims -some forty five percent- two of whom have their heads covered while playing, and sixty percent are Christians but they are one team. These young women sit together and strategize about how they will position themselves to win a game, and keep training to stay at the top. They develop plans and work as a team to achieve their goals. This is a political statement! For me, this image of a female soccer team is my image and my hope for Christians, Muslims and Jews in the Middle East.

Endnotes:

Chapter 2

1. Thus described by Rudi Paret in Mohammed und der Koran, Stuttgart, Berlin, Cologne and Mainz 2/1996.P 9
2. For more on this see Graf, Geschichte der arabisch-christlichen Literatur, part one p15. And Irfan Shahid, "Ghasan" in The Encyclopedia of Islam, the second new edition. p 1020. J Spencer Trimingham, Christianity among the Arabs in PreIslamic Times Longman. London and New York. And Librarie du Liban, published in London 1979. p. 178-188
3. For more on this. See Graf. Part One. p.18 and Irfan Shahid, "The Lakhmids" the new edition. El-V. pp. 632-634
4. There are a few reliable sources that describe Abraha. According to Procopius, the Ethiopian King, Hellestheaios occupied the south of the Arabian Peninsula in the second quarter of the sixth century. He killed the Yemenite king, and appointed in his place an Ethiopian called Esinphaios. He did not remain long in this position because the Ethiopians who settled in the south of the Arabian Peninsula rebelled, succeeded in deposing him, and appointed Abraha to the throne in his place. These events are not entirely clear. It is probable that he was a slave of one of the Byzantine merchants from Adulis. He was famous for restoring the Ma'rib Dam in 657. The Islamic sources explain his attack on Mecca by saying that he wanted to destroy Ka'ba so that the church he built in Sana' would replace Al- Ka'aba as a pilgrimage place. For more on this see A.F.L Beetson. "Abraha", new edition El-1 p 102, and L.I Conrad. "Abraha and Muhammed: some observations apropos of chronology and literary topics in the early Arabic historical tradition". BSOA8. 1987. pp. 225-240.
5. Compare Philip Hilti, History of Syria which includes Lebanon and Palestine, London and New York 1957/2 and The Near East in History; the History of 5000 Years. Princeton, New York. Toronto and London; and George Ostrogorsky. The History of the Byzantine State. Munchen, 1963/3.
6. M.J. Kister, "Mecca and the Tribes of Arabia", in:(id.) "Society and Religion from Jahiliyva to Islam. Vermont/Variorum, 1990, p. 37.
7. T. Noeldeke. Geschichte des Qorans, the first part. Hildesheim/New York: Geor Olms Publisher, p. 74.
8. Compare also Philippe Gignoux in Le doctrines Eschatologiques de Narsai published in Vernon. 1966 L' Orient Syrien(11), pp. 321-352 and pp. 461-488, and also part(12) 1967, pp. 23-54.

9. Islamic history has transmitted one of these Arab Christians sermons as attributed to Qass Ibn Sa'ida. Although what we know about this personality is shrouded in ambiguity, no one doubts his existence(he is mentioned in this article).
10. For more on this sec T. Noeldeke, Part I p. 149, etc.
11. For more on this see B. Holmberg, "Nasturiyyun "new edition, EI-VII pp. 1030-1033; and W. Hage The Influence p. 12, and the Church Condition p. 10; and Graf in The History Geschichte p. 70; and J.S. Trirningham p. 159.
12. Review B. Heiler, Die morgenlaendischen Kirchen, Leiden and Koln, 1964, p.421.
13. F. Riliet "Syriac" in Encyclopedia of the Early Church, part II p. 809.
14. See also S.J. Voicu "The Armenian Language and its Literature", in Encyclopedia of the Early Church, Oxford University Press, New York, 1992, p. 579.
15. In the Persian Empire there were a small number of Monophysite Syrian denominations that did not join the Nestorian Church. Two independent bishoprics supervised these denominations. The center of one bishopric was Mattai Monastery(Mtay) and the other was the city of Taghrit on the Tigris. The relationship of these bishoprics with the Armenian Church was good and lasted for a considerable length of time since the latter was also within die Persian Empire. The union of these denominations with the Syrian Jacobite Church was not consummated until 629, after Heraclaius occupied the Persian Empire. For more on this, see Hage *The Church Condition*, p. 13.
16. Islamic traditions tell of the meeting of Muhammad with a monk called Bahira. This was in Busra in Transjodan. The meeting took place when Muhammad was between nine and thirteen years old when he accompanied his uncle Abu Taleb or Abu Bakr during a voyage to Syria. In this meeting the monk prophesied about the call of Muhammad and warned him of the Jews and the Byzantines. This story questions the defense that even if the Torah did not prophesize about the call of Muhammad it is an indication that Muhammad derived his teachings from Christians who were heretical Christians. The word "Bahira" means in Syriac "the chosen" or "elected." Its owner was either an Arian or Nestorian, or Monophysite. The various viewpoints depend on this information. See also A. Abel, Bahira, the new edition I, 1960, and p. 922, etc.
17. All Qur'anic texts that talk about monks are of Medinan origin. Monastism is mentioned only once in Surat Al-Hadid 57:27: "Then we sent on their wake, Jesus son of Mary, and gave him the Gospel. We put in the hearts of those who followed him kindness and mercy, a monk system that they innovated but that we did not impose on them except seeking God's satisfaction. They did not preserve the right of caring for it. We gave those of them who believed their

reward, and many of them are dissolute". However, there is considerable controversy about the interpretation of this verse. Monks were mentioned twice: once in a negative way, Surat 9: 31-34,"They look their bishops and monks as lords, without taking God as the Lord... O, you who has believed in many bishops and monks eat the money of people..." and another time in a positive way. Surat 5: 87, no. 77 which says: "Say, O, people of the Book, don't say in your religion except that which is true, and don't follow the inclination of a people who were misguided before and they misguided many, and they went astray from the right path. Number 78 says: "Those who became infidel from among the Israelites are cursed on the tongue of David and Jesus son of Mary, because they disobeyed and they were aggressive."For more on this, A J. Wensink, the topic, "Rahbaniyya", EI-VII p. 396, and the same author "rahib" EI- VII p. 397.

18. For more on this see M. Naldini, "Egypt" in EEC I, p. 264; and I.H Dalmais, in"Egypt"(II Liturgy) in: T. Orlandi, in "Coptic" in EEC I p. 199 etc.

19. For more on this see F. Buhl, "Maria" in El, New Ed. VI, 1991, p. 575 and AS. Atiya, "Kipt" in New Ed. V, pp. 90-95.

20. The Islamic historian, Ibn Ishaq, tells us that a Coptic carpenter had built the roof of Al-Ka'aba in 605. See H. Busse p. 12.

21. This is what has been written by S. Trimingham p. 289.

22. For more on this, see O. Raineri, "Ethiopia-Ethiopic" published in EEC I, p. 289.

23. E. Van Dozel, "Al-Najashi" in El New Ed. VII p. 862 etc, and W. Montgomery Watt "Habash-Habasha" in EI New Ed. III 1972, p. II. [24]Compare W. Raven in "Some Early Islamic texts on the Negus of Abyssinia "published in J. S.S. 1988, p. 197 etc.

25. For details on this topic see, J. S. Trimingham, Christianity and Casper Detlef Gustan Mueller, Kirche und Mission unter den Arabern in vorislamischer Zeit. (Sammlung gemeinverstaendlicher Vortraege und Schriften aus dem Gebiet der Theologie und Religionsgeschichte). Tubingen. 1967.

26. References: see no. 2 of comments and explanation.

27. "The word "patriarch" should not be understood here as it is known in the Church. The Byzantine Caesar, Justinian, in 529 gave the title Patricos to Al-Harith and this title appear in early Arabic literature on the Patriarch. See J.S. Triminham. p. 180.

28. See 'Irfan Shadid; "Byzantino-Arabica. The Conference of Ramla, A.D. 524, published in the *Journal of Middle Eastern Studies* number 23. 1964. pp. 115-131.

29. It is worthwhile to mention here Al-Nabigha Al-Dhubyani. Abu Daoud Al-Ayadi. Aws Ibn Hajjar. Jurair Ibn Abdul-Messih and Maynoun ibn Qays, known as al- 'Aasha. See also: J.S. Trimingham p. 201.
30. One of the references. J.S. Trimingham p. 223.
31. The legend of the Arian historian Philostrogius has historical significance. This legend tells of the conversion of the Saba'ians to Christianity by Theofelous, the emissary of the Byzantine Caesar, Justinian. For more on this, see J.S. Trimingham p. 292.
32. This was what the Arian historian Philostrogius(360-430) told. He wrote: "Costantius sent ambassadors to those who were formerly called Saba'ians and are now known as Homeritae. They are a tribe descended from Abraham by his wife Katura. As for the region they inhabit, he says that the Yowanians call it Arabia Felix. It extends to the furthest limits of the Ocean and its capital is Saba." Conveyed by J.S. Trimingham, p. 292.
33. See J.S. Trimingham, p. 292.
34. See al-'Aasha(died in 629) in his collection of poetry, and see also J.S Trimingham, p. 305.
35. For further discussion see T. Noeldeke I p. 97.
36. Conveyed by J.S. Trimingham, p. 306.
37. This is a reliable story told by A. Baumstark in "The Problem of Christian Church Writings in the Arabic Language before Islam", published in the magazine Islamic 1931; pp. 562-575.
38. Refer to Ebenda p. 565.
39. Among those worth mentioning here are: Louis Shikho, *Christianity and Its Literature in the Jahiliyyah Arabs*, published in Beirut, 1923; and Abdul-Messih Al-Maqdisi, *Translating the Holy Books into Arabic before Islam*, published in Al- Mashreq, no. 31, 1933, pp. 1-12: and Khalil Samir, *The Characteristics of the Ancient Christian Arab Heritage*, published in Theological Review V/2, 1982, pp. 156-190. Other references include Wakil Hakim "Fr. Louis Shikho and the images of Christianity in Al-Jahiliyya" published in *Al-Mashreq* no. 64, 1970, pp. 297-322. One of the most important supporters of this school of thought in our present age is 'Irfan Shadid. Even if he built his supposition on guessing, he believes that in the fourth century there were very simple Arabic rituals and Arabic translations of the most important scripture readings which aid the liturgy. He goes further and talks about the establishment of an Arab Church that followed the Patriarchate of Antioch in the fourth century. References: 'Irfan Shadid in Roma and the Arabs: A Prolegomenon to the Study of Byzantium and the Arabs published by Dumbarton Oaks Research Library and

Collection. Washington. D.C 1984, and the same author in *"Byzantium and the Arabs in the fourth century"*, Dumbarton Oaks. Washington. D.C. 1984. See especially pp. 435-443 and 554-558 and the same author in Byzantium and the Arabs in the 5th Century. Dumbarton Oaks. Washington. D.C. 1989. Review especially pp. 422-457 and 520-528.

40. Among those who strongly defended the existence of Christian Arab literature before Islam was W, Rudolph, Die Abhaengigkeit des Qorans vom Judentum und Christenlum. Stuttgart 1922: T. Andrae. Der Ursprung des Islams und das Christentum. Uppsala/Stockholm. 1926: K. Ahrens. Christliches im Qoran' in: Zeitschrift der Deulschen Morgcnlaendischen Gesellschafl 84(1930). S. 15-68 und 177-201: and also especially A. Baunstark. „The Sunday Evangelism in Jerusalem before the Byzantine Period" published in Byzantine Publications(30). 1919-1920. pp. 350-359: A. Baunstark, „Problem of the Christian Church Writings in the Arabic Language before Islam" published in Islamica 4, 1931. pp. 562-575: A. Baunstark. „An ancient Arabic translation of the Gospels translated from the Christian Palestinian" published in Senistik 8. 1932. pp. 201-209: A. Baunstark. „From the Preserved Texts: the most Ancient Text of Psalm 110(109) Greek/Arabic, published in the Magazine *Oriens Christianus.* no. 31. 1934. pp.55-66; A. Baunstark, "The translation of the Gospels in Arabic from the Dawn of Islam: Another Translation before Islam" published in "Atti" del XIX Congresso Internazionale Degli Orientalisti Rome 1938, pp. 682-684. The scholar Joshua Blau a Scholar in Semitics and its literature, expressed his opposition to Baiernstark's latter theory, Sind uns Reste arabischer Bibeluebersetzungen aus vorislamischer Zeit erhalten geblieben? Published *in Le Museon* number 86. 1973. pp. 67-72.

41. See J.S. Trimingbanm:"Christianity"

42. See Hage. "The Influence"(Einfluss).

43. Review C. Rabin: "Arabiyya: The Arabic Language" which appears in EI new Ed. p564. The Islamic historian Al-Tabari told the following story: "After Khalid Ibn Al-Waleed made an agreement with the Anbars, he noticed that they wrote in Arabic with supreme skill. He asked them: "Who are you?" They replied: "We are an Arab group that arc descended from one of the Arab tribes that was here before and whose ancestors settled in this country at the time of Nabukhadnassar who wanted to settle the Arabs. We have continued to live here. "He then asked: "Who taught you the letters?" They answered him: "We learned writing from Iyad." This was told by J.S. Trimingham. pg. 227.

44. Review Ebenda

45. The initiative in the first translation of the Gospels from the Syriac language into Arabic was an Islamic initiative. This is based on the traditions passed

down, which indicated that the Muslim ruler 'Amr Ibn Sa'd Abi Waqqas requested an Arabic translation from the Antiochian Patriarch Yuhanna Al-Sadrawi. As the Patriarch did not know Arabic, he sought the help of Christian Arabs in Tayy and Al-Hira(they were Lakhmids) However, this translation no longer exists. But the oldest translation, which has been preserved, is a translation of the Psalms, which date to around the ninth century. Compare J.S. Trimingham, p. 225.

46. It was transmitted by W. Hage, Der Einfluss des orientalischen Christentums auf den werdenden Islam, in: Willi Hofner(Ed.). *Der Islam als nachchristliche Religion*, published by Christian Jensen Breklum, LTD. 1971. For more on Qass Bin Saida, see the chapter "Pellat" on the topic "Qass Bin Saida." published in EI New Ed. V, Brill Leiden. 1986. p.529.

Chapter 3

1. For his classic article dealing with this subject, see "Is the Qur'an the Word of God?"(Smith, 1981: 282-300). For his fuller elaboration of this approach, Smith, 1993: 21-44.
2. Das Koranische Jesusbild, Helsinki, 1971.
3. Christianity and the World Religions: Paths to Dialogue with Islam, Hinduism, and Buddhism. London: Collins, 1985.
4. See Raheb(1995), especially the chapter "My identity as a Palestinian Christian", pp. 3-14.
5. (Raheb, 1995: 9).
6. (Ibid.: 10-11)
7. (Ibid: 4-6)
8. (Ibid.: 44)
9. (Arkoun, 1992)
10. (Q12:2 et passim)
11. (Noldeke, 1970: 7)
12. (Fahd: 420)
13. (Q52, 29; Q69, 41; Q37, 35)
14. (Q111)
15. (Q106)
16. (Q75, 18)

Endnotes 133

17 (Q74, 49-56; Q69, 47)
18 (Q97, 3)
19 (Q87: 18; Q53: 37-54)
20 (Pellat: 537); see Q26,123-40; Q11,52-63; Q7,63-70 et passim for the main features of Hud's story among the people of 'Ad between modern-day Uman and Hadramawt in Southern Arabia.
21 See Q7: 73; Q11: 61 Q26:141; Q51:43; Q54: 24; Q69:4; Q27: 45 for the story of Salih's mission among the people of Thamud, in Northern Arabia.
22 (Q69: 4-6); see Q11: 89; Q26: 176-89; Q50: 13; Q15: 78; Q3: 13; Q11: 84-95; Q29: 36 for the story of Shu'aib's mission among the Medianites. He may be identified with Yethro in the Hebrew scriptures.
23 (Guillaume, 1978: 146)
24 (Q5: 85-6)
25 (Q19)
26 (Paret. 1975:175)
27 In contrast to modern usage of this term, the qur'anic term denotes a tribe or clan, or a group of people who accept a common patriarchal leader, with a common genealogy, and shared locality. In this latter sense it may denote a city-state.
28 (Q35: 24; Q14: 4; Q10: 47)
29 (Q11)
30 These letters are an example of the phenomenon of consonantal prefixes which appear at the beginning of thirty suras of the Qur'an. They are known as the "abbreviated letters"(al-muqatta'at), the meaning and function of which are unclear.
31 (Q11: 1-2)
32 (Q11: 3-4)
33 (Q11: 25-26)
34 (Q11: 50-95)...
35 (Q11: 96-109)
36 I coin this term in preference over Johann Fueck's characterization of the Qur'anic concept of revelation being "cyclic"; see Paret, 1995: 175.
37 (Busse, 1988: 102)
38 For example, the story of the creation and sin: 7, 11-25, 15, 26-4§; 17, 61-65; 2i 116-124; 38, 71; 11, 69-76; 15, 51-56; 19, 41-50; 21, 51-72; 26, 69-86; 37, 83-113; 4: 26; 51: 24-37; of Joseph(above all sura 12); of Moses: 7, 104-162;

10, 75-82; 11, 17, 10 19, 51-53; 20, 9-98; 26,10-68; 27, 7-12; 28,1-50; 40, 23-46; of David: 17, 55; 21, 78; 2 15; 34, 10; 38, 18-25; and Solomon: 21, 81; 27, 15-44; 34, 12; 38, 30-40. Other verse relate to the New Testament stories, which stem most of the time from Medina(3, 33-5' 4, 157-158; 5, 110-120).

39 (Q12: 111; Q26: 196; Q46: 12)
40 (Q32: 3; Q36: 6)
41 (Q34: 44)
42 (Q34: 44)
43 (Bowman, 1981: 31-8)
44 (Graham, 1987: 90)
45 (Ibid: 45); see also Smith, W. 1993.
46 (Neuwirth, 1981: 1-10)
47 (Q7: 204)
48 (Neuwirth, 1991: 331-57)
49 (Q12: 2; Q13: 37; Q41: 44; Q42: 7; ,jQ43: 30)
50 (Q41)
51 (Q41: 44).
52 (Q12: 2; Q20: 113; Q41: 3; Q42: 3; Q26: 198)
53 (Smith, 1981: 244)
54 (Q19: 58)
55 (Paret, 1975: 83)
56 (Q14: 4)
57 (Q17: 93)
58 (Guillaume, 1978: 192)
59 (Q3: 23; Q4: 44, 51)
60 The Arabic word injil probably derives from the Ethiopian term wangel and should therefore be differentiated etymologically from the Greek euangelion. The term is used twelve times in the Qur'an, exclusively in Medinan chapters.
61 (Q5:13; Q2: 75; Q4: 46; Q5: 41)
62 (Q3: 3; Q4: 105; Q5: 51)
63 (Q2: 80, 94, 111; Q3: 24; Q4: 49; Q5: 18)
64 (ummiyyun: Q3: 75)
65 (Noldeke, 1970: 159)
66 (Q7: 157)

Endnotes

67 (Q2:129)
68 (Q6: 61)
69 (John 14: 16-17; 16: 7-11)
70 (Q6: 86; Q21: 85)
71 (Q2: 124-128)
72 See especially Genesis 16, 17, and 21: 9-21.
73 (Hayek, 1964)
74 (Q2, 136; Q3, 84)
75 For a discussion of the difference between Muslim and Christian views of Jesus, see Neal Robinson, Christ in Islam and Christianity(1991).
76 (Watt: 165).
77 (Q6: 74-82; Q19: 41-50)
78 (Q2: 135)
79 (Q3: 65-67)
80 (Q6: 161-163)
81 (Q106)
82 (Q2: 124-129)
83 (as Q2:127 might suggest)
84 (as suggested by Q2: 125)
85 (Q2: 128)
86 (Q2: 129)
87 (imam li'l-nass: Q2: 124)

Chapter 4

1. This summary is based basically on the author's dissertation. Mitri Raheb Das reformatorische Erbe unter den Palaestinensern, (Die Lutherische Kirche. Geschichte und Gestalten, Bd.11) Gueterslon 1990.

2. More here to: E. Benze, Wittenberg und Byzanz Marburg 1949; E. Benz a. L.A. Zander, Evangelisches und Orthodox Christentum in Begegnung und Auseinandersetzung, Hamburg 1952.

3. For details: D. Wendebourg, Reformation und Orthodoxoxie, Geottingen 1986; Wort und Mysterium. Der Briefwechsel ueber Glauben und Kirche 1573 bis

1581 zwichen den Tuebinger Thologen und dem Patriarchen von Konstantinopel, Witten 1958.
4. Peter Kawerau, Amerika unde die orientalischen Christen. Ursprung und Afgang der Amerikanischen Mission unter den Nationalkirchen Asiens, Berlin 1958, p. 171.
5. A. L. Tibawi, British Interests in Palestine 1800 – 1901. A Study of Religious and Educational Enterprise, Oxford 1961, p. 12.
6. Kawerau, p. 173.
7. Tibawi, p.12.
8. Ibid, p. 9.
9. A.R. Sinno, Deutshe Interessen in Syrian und Palastina 1841 – 1898. Aktivitaelen religioeser Institutionen, wirtschaftliche und politishe Einfluesse (Studien zum modernen islamischen Orient, Bd. 3), Berlin 1982, p. 11
10. Tibawi, p. 16
11. Ibid, p. 16
12. Ibid, p. 14
13. For details: Moshe Maoz, Ottoman Reform in Syria and Palestine 1840 – 1861. The Impact of the Tanzimat on Politics and Society, London 1968.
14. H. Abeken a. C.K.J. Bunsen, Das Evangelishe Bisthum in Jerusalem. Geschichtliche Darlegung mit Urkunden, Berlin 1842.
15. Ibid. pp. 33-41.
16. Daphne Tsimhoni, The British Mandate and the Arab Christians in Palestine 1920-1925, London 1967 (unpublished dissertation), p. 109.
17. Tibawi, p. 79
18. Abeken, p. 34.
19. Raheb, p. 105.
20. Tibawi, p. 84.
21. J. Roi, Michael Salomon Alexander, der erste evangelische Bischof von Jerusalem. Ein Beitrag zur orientalischen Frage (Schriften des Institutum Judaicum in Berlin, 22), Guetersloh 1897.
22. Raheb, pp. 39-41.
23. Ibid., pp. 42-58.
24. Ibid., pp. 42-45.
25. Ibid. p. 50.
26. Ibid. , p. 51.

27. Ibid., p. 54.
28. Ibid. p. 55.
29. Ibid., p56.
30. Ibid.
31. Ibid., p. 81.
32. Ibid., pp. 59-61.
33. Ibid., pp. 62-77.
34. Ibid., pp. 78-81.
35. Ibid. pp. 89-95.
36. Ibid.,pp. 95-98.
37. Ibid.,pp. 113-116.
38. Ibid. , pp. 110 – 112.
39. Tibawi, p. 215.
40. Raheb, pp. 99-104.
41. Ibid. p. 106.
42. Ibid. pp. 125- 185.
43. Ibid., pp. 142 -144.
44. Ibid., pp. 189 – 212.
45. Ibid., p. 192.
46. Ibid. p, 203
47. Ibid., p. 204
48. Ibid., p. 189.
49. Ibid., pp. 205 – 212.
50. Hanna Issa, Love in action >In His Service<. The story of the Lutheran World Federation in the Middle East, Jerusalem, 1970, p. 22.
51. Raheb, pp. 213 -227
52. Ibid., pp. 246- 248.
53. Mitri Raheb, Ich bin Christ und Palestinenser, Israel, seine Nachbarn und die Bible, Guetersloh 1994, p. 77.
54. Ibid. .
55. Ibid.,p.78.
56. Ibid.,pp.81-110.
57. Ibid, p. 75
58. Ibid., p.76

Selectd Bibliography

Chapter 3

- Arkoun, A. 1982. Lectures au Coran, Paris: Maisonneuve & Larose.
- Bowman, J. 1980. "Holy scriptures, lectionaries and the Koran", in International Congress for the Study of the Koran,(ed.) Johns. Canberra: Australian National University.
- Busse, H. 1988. Die Theologischen Beziehungen des Islams zu Judentum und Christentun Grundlagen des Dialogs im Koran und die Gegenwaertige Situation. Darmstadt: Wissen schaftliche Buchgesellschaft.
- Fahd, T. „Kahin" in Encyclopaedia of Islam(New Edition), Vol. IV.
- Graham, W. 1987. Beyond the Written Word: Oral Aspects of Scripture in the History of Religion. Cambridge: Cambridge University Press.
- Guillaume, A. 1978. The Life of Muhammad: a Translation of In Ishaq's Sirat Rasul Allah. London: Oxford University Press.
- Hayek, M. 1964. Le Mystere d'Ismael. Paris: Maison Mame.
- Neuwirth, A. 1981. Studien zur Komposition der Mekkanischen Suren. Berlin/ New York Walter de Gruyter.
- Neuwirth, A& C. 1991. "Surat al Fatiha: 'Eroeffnung' des Text-Corpus Koran ode Introitus' der Gebetsliturgie?", in Text, Methode und Grammatih,(eds) Walter Gross Hubert Irsigler, Th Seidel, St Ottilien: Eos Verlag.
- Noldeke, Th. 1970. Geschichte des Qorans. Hildesheim/New York: Geor Olms Publisher.
- Paret, R. 1975. Der Koran. Darmstadt: Wissenschaftliche Buchgesellschaft.
- Raheb, M . 1995. I am a Palestinian Christian. Minneapolis: Fortress Press.
- Robinson, N. 1991. Christ in Islam and Christianity: the Representation of Jesus in the Qur'an and the Classical Muslim Commentaries. London: Macmillan Press.
- Smith, WC. 1981. On Understanding Islam. The Hague: Mouton Publishers..
- Id., 1993. What is Scripture? a Comparative Approach. Minneapolis: Fortress Press.
- Watt, WM. 1990. Early Islam: Collected Articles. Edinburgh: Edinburgh University Press.
- Id., 1961. Muhammad: Prphet and Statesman. London: Oxford University Press.

Chapter 5

1. Raheb, Mitri. I am a Palestinian Christian, Minneapolis: Augsburg Fortress Press, 1995.
2. Viola Raheb (Ed.), Latin American with Palestinian Roots.(Bethlehem: Diyar 2012)
3. Johnny Mansour, Arab Christians in Israel: Facts, Figures and Trends. (Bethlehem: Diyar 2012)
4. Rania Al Qass Collings, Rifat Odeh Kassis and Mitri Raheb, Palestinian Christians in the West Bank: Facts, Figures and Trends.(Bethlehem: Diyar 2012)
5. Mitri Raheb, Bethlehem Besieged: Stories of Hope at Times of Fear. (Minneapolis: Fortress 2004).
6. Khoury, Geries. Guide to the Church in the Holy Land. Nazareth: 1984.
7. Winkelman, Friedhelm. Die oestlichen Kirchen in der Epoche der christologischen Auseinandersetzungen.(Kirchengeschichte in Einzeldarstellungen I/6, ed. Gert Haendle et al.). Berlin: 1983.
8. Attwater, Donald. The Uniate Churches of the East. London: Geoffrey Chapman, 1961.
9. Etteldorf, Raymond. The Catholic Church in the Middle East. New York: Macmillan, 1959.
10. Raheb, Mitri. Das reformatorische Erbe unter den Palaestinensern, zur Entstehung der Evangelisch-Lutherischen Kirche in Jordanien. Guetersloh: Guetersloher Verlaghaus, 1990.
11. Rania Al Qass Collings, Palestinian Christians, p. 16-31.
12. Sennott, Charles. The Body and the Blood. The Holy Land's Christians at the Turn of a New Millennium. A Reporter's Journey. New York: Public Affairs, 2001.
13. Cragg, Kenneth. The Arab Christian. A History in the Middle East. Louisville: Westminster/John Knox Press, 1991.
14. Griffith, Sidney. Arabic Christianity in the Monasteries of Ninth-Century Palestine. Collected Studies, CS380. Aldershot & Brookfield, VT: Variorum, 1992.
15. Hourani, Albert. Arabic Thought in the Liberal Age, 1789-1939. Cambridge: 1983.
16. Aburish, Said. The Forgotten Faithful: The Christians of the Holy Land. London: Quartet Books, 1993.

17. Adalah: The Legal Center Legal for Arab Minority rights in Israel. <u>Violations of Arab Minority Rights in Israel</u>, Schefa'amr: 1998.
18. Kjaer-Hansen, K. - Kvarme, O. <u>Messianische Juden. Judenchristen in Israel</u>, Erlangen: Ev. Luth. Verlaghaus, 1979.
19. "The Palestinian Authority's Treatment of Christians in the Autonomous Areas," Report from the Prime Ministers office, October 1997.

About the Auther

Dr. Mitri Raheb is the President of Diyar Consortium and of Dar al-Kalima University College in Bethlehem, as well as the president of the Synod of the Evangelical Lutheran Church in Jordan and the Holy Land in addition to being the Senior Pastor of the Evangelical Lutheran Christmas Church in Bethlehem, Palestine. The most widely published Palestinian theologian to date, Dr. Raheb is the author of 16 books including: Das Reformatorische Erbe unter den Palaestinensern, I am a Palestinian Christian; Bethlehem Besieged. He is the Chief Editor of the Contextual Theology Series at Diyar Publishing including: The Invention of History, A Century of Interplay between Theology and Politics in Palestine; The Biblical Text in the Context of Occupation: Towards a new hermeneutics of liberation. His books and numerous articles have been translated so far into eleven languages.

The 50 year-old multilingual contextual theologian received for his 'distinguished service to church and society' the prestigious Wittenberg Award from the Luther Center in DC (2003). He also received for his 'outstanding contribution to Christian education through research and publication' an honorary doctorate from Concordia University in Chicago (2003) and for his 'interfaith work toward peacemaking in Israel and Palestine' the "International Mohammad Nafi Tschelebi Peace Award" of the Central Islam Archive in Germany (2006) and in 2007 the well-known German Peace Award of Aachen. In 2012 the German Media Prize, a Prize granted mainly to head of states, was awarded to Dr. Raheb for his "tireless work in creating room for hope for his people, who are living under Israeli Occupation, through founding and building institutions of excellence in education, culture and health."

The work of Dr. Raheb has received wide media attention from major international media outlets and networks including CNN, ABC, CBS, 60 Minutes, BBC, ARD, ZDF, DW, BR, Premiere, Raiuno, Stern, The Economist, Newsweek, and Vanity Fair.

Dr. Raheb holds a Doctorate in Theology from the Philipps University at Marburg, Germany. He is married to Najwa Khoury and has two daughters, Dana & Tala. For more, www.mitriraheb.org